NATIONAL POLICY RESPONSES TO URBAN GROWTH

For Marcia, Chris and Gaby

National Policy Responses to Urban Growth

PHILIP. H. FRIEDLY

SAXON HOUSE | LEXINGTON BOOKS

Published by

SAXON HOUSE, D. C. Heath Ltd.
Westmead, Farnborough, Hants., England.

Jointly with

LEXINGTON BOOKS, D. C. Heath & Co.
Lexington, Mass. U.S.A.

ISBN 0 347 01061 X
Library of Congress Catalog Card Number 74-7642
Printed in Great Britain by Robert MacLehose and Company Limited
Printers to the University of Glasgow

Contents

Preface   xiii

PART I   INTRODUCTION   1

   1   Some Common Policy Concerns   3
   2   Purpose and Structure of the Study   9

PART II   MODELS AND ANALYSES TO GUIDE POLICY APPLI-
CATION   13

   3   The Objects of Policy: Working Definitions of Urban Areas
      and Growth Sectors   15
       Area definitions for urban policy analysis   18
       Growth sectors: the urban shift to quaternary functions
         and geographic centrality   31

   4   Trends and Hypotheses in Urban Growth and Distribution   39
       Major features of the growth trends   40
       Geographic shifts by offices and quaternary functions:
         changing opportunity structures   53
   5   National Policy Responses and Feasible Implementation Stra-
      tegies   73
       The emerging urban growth policy focus as reflected in
         national goals   73
       Some analytical constructs for policy development and
         assessment   77
       Sampling national policy responses: Great Britain, France
         and the United States   94

PART III   TYPES AND USE OF INSTRUMENTS: EXAMPLES OF
INNOVATION IN POLICY IMPLEMENTATION   119

   6   Classification of the Range of Instruments Available   121
       Generic types of policy instruments   121
       Patterns of instrument use by type   125
   7   Infrastructure Guidance and Control   147
       Transport in Greater London   147

Infrastructural allocations in France   156
Infrastructural reinforcement for urban expansion in the
   Netherlands   161
8   Government and Private Office Location Guidance   163
   Relocating government offices from London   163
   Government office relocations from Stockholm   173
   Government voluntary consultations with private enter-
      prise in Sweden   179
   Experimenting with government office relocation from
      Bonn   181

PART IV   CONCLUDING PERSPECTIVES AND FUTURE IMPLI-
CATIONS   187
9   Private Decisions and Public Policy Planning   189
10   Some Clues to Location and Life Style Preferences 193
11   Migration, Growth and Dislocation: Some Questions of
     Equity   201
12   Conclusions: State of the Art and Future Lines of Advance 213

Index   219

List of figures

3.1   The Assisted Areas in Great Britain, 1972   16
3.2   Passenger commuter traffic by rail in the Randstad, 1959   17
3.3   Spheres of influence of cities in France   19
3.4   The city-region of Frankfurt: newspaper circulations of the
      central places   20
3.5   The city-region of Frankfurt: commuting to selected cities in
      Hesse, 1950   21
3.6   Gradients of urban influence in the United States, 1960   23
3.7   Principal activity regions in England and Wales, 1966   25
3.8   Holiday/retirement regions in England and Wales   26
3.9   Administrative/market regions in England and Wales   27
3.10 The growth of Stockholm between 1850 and 1966   29
3.11 Population of three major US cities at different dates, accord-
      ing to different city boundaries   30

3.12 North-eastern urban complex in relation to the whole United
States, 1960   31

4.1 Comparison of projections for Greater London   43

4.2 Comparisons of projections for the Outer Metropolitan Area   44

4.3 Comparison of projections for the Outer South East   45

4.4 Population distribution by national zones, 1870–1970   46

4.5 Net migration flows to the three metropolitan regions of Sweden, 1966   47

4.6 Relationship of the population growth rate of USA daily urban systems, 1960–70, to their size in 1960   51

4.7 Destination of office jobs moved from Greater London through the Location of Offices Bureau 1963–71   55

4.8 The contact system – a summary   58

4.9 The spatial contact pattern in Sweden   60

4.10 The relationship between income level and business journeys, in Sweden   61

4.11 The relationship between income level and time spent on contact activity, in Sweden   62

5.1 Example of multiplier leverage   78

5.2 Inter-plant linkage classification   79

5.3 Rates of employment change in Great Britain, 1959–69   81

5.4 Spatial association: old industries in Great Britain   82

5.5 Spatial association: new industries in Great Britain   82

5.6 Inter-sectoral contact flows and office clusters in Central London, 1973   84

5.7 How migratory motives change with social progress   91

5.8 Schematic representation of the relationship between the 'well-being' of migrants, those they leave behind and those they join, with special reference to the related size of the various populations   94

5.9 The causes of increasing journey-to-work distances   95

5.10 South East Region in England   96

5.11 Employment imbalances in London in 1966   97

5.12 Indices of commuting independence in S.E. England in 1966 by distance from Central London   99

5.13 Indices of commuting independence for towns within 35 miles of London by size 100

5.14 Journeys to work in five British new town areas in 1966 by socio-economic group 101

5.15 Rapidly developing towns in England and Wales 103

5.16 Population of urbanised areas ranked by size, and change in rank of four selected cities in ranking of cumulative number of places by size in the United States, 1790–1950 104

5.17 Growth restraints in Great Britain 105

5.18 Urbanisation in Great Britain. Regional distribution of urban land, recent increases and restraints to future development ... 108

5.19 Green Belts in South East England, 1968 110

5.20 Major recreational facilities and Areas of Outstanding Natural Beauty in South East England, 1968 111

5.21 Urban growth strategy map for France 112

5.22 Distribution of support for tertiary sector activity in France ... 113

5.23 Zones under the Paris Region office development tax 114

6.1 Infrastructure decisions in Sweden 142

6.2 Infrastructure co-ordination in the Netherlands 143

7.1 Existing and committed primary roads and motorways in Greater London, 1970 149

7.2 Primary road networks in selected large cities 150

7.3 Peak and off-peak journey speeds and parking control in Central London 154

7.4 The pattern of central government infrastructure and related assistance in France, 1966–70 157

7.5 Routes operated by Air-Inter in France, 1965–71 158

7.6 Air routes in France opening during 1972 159

8.1 Office development permits in South East England, 1966–72 174

8.2 Central government organisation for the execution of relocalisation of government departments in Sweden 175

8.3 Executive plan for relocalisation from Stockholm of various government departments to Norrköpping 177

10.1 Distribution and degree of preference for places in West Germany as business locations, 1970–71 194

10.2 Distribution and degree to which places are disliked in West Germany, 1970–71   195

List of tables

3.1 Average size of United States metropolitan areas, by region, 1900 and 1960   28

3.2 Percentage distribution of gross domestic product, 1951–52 and 1961–62   32

3.3 Changes in office and other workers in employment by industry group, England and Wales, 1951–61   33

3.4 Growth in managerial and clerical employment in England and Wales 1961–66   34

3.5 Production and employment by type of economic activity in the period 1961–70   35

3.6 Employment in different branches of services in the period 1961–70   35

3.7 Employment structure (percentages) of Greater London, South East Standard Region, and England and Wales, 1951 to 1969 by workplace   36

4.1 Change in English conurbation populations, 1951 to 1966   41

4.2 Mid-year estimates of resident population   42

4.3 Evolution of the population of Paris and France, 1801–1965   48

4.4 The population of the Paris agglomeration   48

4.5 Population change in the major agglomerations of the Paris Basin by growth rates and distance from Paris   49

4.6 Population change in the major agglomerations of France, 1962–68   50

4.7 Distances moved by decentralisers from Central London, 1963–69   54

4.8 Mobile industry within South East England: transfer of employees by distance of move and type of employment, 1945–68   56

4.9 Changes in managerial and clerical employment, Greater London, 1961—66   57

4.10 The contact-intensity of industrial, trade and service sectors and the regional concentration of employment   59

4.11 Sweden: income distribution, 1967   64

4.12 Population and jobs, by parts of the New York region, 1956 and 1965   66

4.13 Major industries increasingly concentrated in Manhattan, 1967 and 1969   67

4.14 Value added per employee, United States and New York SMSA, by major industries in New York SMSA, 1963 and 1967   67

4.15 Industrial productivity by hierarchical level of urban units, standardised for capital intensity, size of firm and size of urban unit, Sweden 1968   68

4.16 Index of per capita income, over time by SMSA population group and region   69

4.17 Deflated money income levels for standardised population, 1966   70

5.1 Supply linkages in Nordrhein—Westfalen   80

5.2 Sources of purchase for major industries in the New York SMSA   85

5.3 Median growth rates of various types of economic areas, 1960—70   86

5.4 Federal expenditure concentration ratios by functional categories for diverse types of areas in the United States, 1969/70   88

5.5 Consumption per member of household in regions at different levels of agglomeration in Sweden   93

5.6 Employment imbalances in the London region in 1966   97

5.7 Employment and population in Central London 1921—66   98

5.8 Indices of commuting independence for London's new towns in 1951, 1961, and 1966   98

5.9 Major restraints on development in Great Britain between 1966 and 1970   106

5.10 Distribution of urban area and policy restraints on growth in Great Britain, 1966—70   107

6.1 Central government measures in European countries   126

6.2 The structure of regional subsidies 1965—71 in Sweden   128

6.3 Unemployment in total labour force for 1971 in different regions of Sweden   128

6.4 Total cash value of investment incentive benefits during the first three years of a project in respect of expenditure for industrial buildings and machinery separately   130

6.5 Current industrial mobility measures in Sweden and the United Kingdom, 1971   135

6.6 Selected Federal programmes of possible assistance for new community growth and public facilities, in the United States, 1967   136

6.7 Classification of regional centres by amenities   141

7.1 Primary road mileage per thousand population in London and selected English cities, 1968   151

7.2 Primary road mileage per million population proposed in selected cities   151

7.3 Percentage of land used for roads in selected major cities   152

7.4 Changes in parking supply and demand, London 1966—71   153

7.5 Changes in parking space supply in the ILPA, 1970—81   153

7.6 Parking standards for offices and shops in Greater London   154

7.7 Changes in road mileage and travel speed in Greater London, 1962—70   155

7.8 Proportionate contribution of direct stimulating and indirect infrastructural measures to total employment growth in the north of the Netherlands, 1960—67   160

8.1 Geographical and functional distribution of central government staff in the United Kingdom   164

8.2   Central government office jobs relocated or scheduled for relocation from London by 1972   165

8.3   Changes in the number of central government employees in different urban areas of Sweden between 1966 and 1970   178

8.4   Alternative rankings of West German cities as candidates for Federal office location   182

10.1   Preferred type of residential location in the event of a household move, West Germany, 1971   197

10.2   Factors needed to be satisfactory before moving in the United Kingdom, 1966   198

11.1   Current taxable value of real property in 1970 and changes in taxable values 1965–70 in Greater London and other selected areas   204

11.2   Changes in population and real property tax rate burdens in Greater London and other selected areas   206

11.3   Changes in household income and its distribution in Greater London and other areas, 1965–70   207

11.4   1980 projections under varying growth assumptions for Santa Clara county   209

Preface

Lay no small plans! admonished the visionary and bold planner of the not too distant past. Lay no plans at all! threatens the disjointed incrementalist of nineteenth-century liberal stripe. Lay plans that are flexible, responsive, and highly leveraged! compromises the pragmatic contemporary policy-maker. We do not merely make jest with these intellectually diverse exhortations. Although they need not always represent honest differences of opinion about the way the world is, or what we ought to do about it, they can and often do. Not being strictly a treatise on moral values, this book has little to say about how things ought to be in a truly good world, even though value judgement on important questions of equity does not escape us. Mainly, we address the questions about the way the world — the urban world in the increasingly post-industrial West European and North American nations — is today and where it is heading for in the future.

The incessantly demanding public issues of economic prosperity and efficiency, social equity, and environmental quality — all ingredients in our quality-of-life index — are bringing conflicting, and often unbearable, pressures on our national policy-makers. Little enough is known about our present trends of urban growth and condition, let alone about where or how we shall be living at the end of the twentieth century. If it is the whole nexus of problems and issues surrounding what we define in the book that follows as urban growth and distribution about which we speak, then the difficulty is one of overwhelming complexity and countervailing forces. In such a case, the planner's inclination might be to attempt to harness the complex beast in a rigid and ossifying framework of control and regulation, i.e. overplanning as we find it in some of the Eastern European nations. The non-planner's inclination might be to become over-whelmed willingly and look to the market mechanism as ultimate arbiter of all these social issues.

But there are things that are known today about urban growth trends and public action alternatives or choices open to society. It is our intention to plumb just this state of knowledge and the nature of the national policy strategies and actions emerging in order to find out how far we have come and to assess where we can and might be headed in our urban growth. Without lapsing into the sometime facile rhetoric of the policy analyst, we can say honestly that the complex subject of urban growth contains many avenues down which to tread. Thus there is a dire need to reduce the multidimensionality of the problem and to focus on the crucial and, yes, leverageable points of intervention consistent with the values extant in mixed-economy and democratic societies that desire to remain relatively free of unnecessary bureaucratic encumbrances.

Because of the paucity of existing efforts to place urban growth and development in useful and operational national policy frameworks, this book lies near the beginning of such a task. Therefore, it constitutes an initial probe into the complex of problems and organisational choices for action open to society. The investigation is conducted comparatively in an international setting with the hope that insights gained across several national experiences will enhance the value of our conclusions.

The author has relied heavily on the assessments and impressions of the many government officials and staff and outside experts who were interviewed personally in their own countries. Without such a feeling and sense of the current policy implementation environment in each country provided through these discussions, in addition to the facts and figures supplied, many of the crucial judgements in this book could not have been formulated. The author expresses his deepest gratitude to each and every person he met, all of whom provided generous amounts of time and great insight into the conditions prevailing in France, the United Kingdom, the Netherlands, Sweden, the Federal Republic of Germany, the United States, Canada, and Spain. The experience of these countries is drawn on selectively in this book as it is relevant to the problems and issues under discussion. It is by no means exhaustive but was limited by the time and resources available to the author. For this reason, considerable relevant experience remains yet to be analysed.

Colleagues and friends in the United States and Europe have read and commented on the manuscript, thereby assisting the author greatly to assess the quality of substance and purpose. Most remain unnamed but a particular debt is due to James Sundquist of the Brookings Institution and William Alonso of the University of California at Berkeley for their constructive criticisms.

Special thanks are due to Lindsay McFarland for perceptive analysis of the experience in France relating to guidance of office locations. Much of what appears in this book on this subject relies on her work. Thanks also are due to Diana Evans for typing of the manuscript, which was handled efficiently and cheerfully under a not small amount of pressure on occasions. These two assisted the author while he was resident in Paris and during the period of field work and writing in Europe.

None of these people nor any of the organisations with whom the author is or has been associated bear any responsibility for the opinions and conclusions that appear in the book that follows. For these the author claims full and sole responsibility.

PART I

Introduction

1 Some Common Policy Concerns

Many economically advanced countries are at present engaged in their own wide-ranging evaluations of national policies relating to urban growth and to the form and structure of urban areas within their respective national boundaries. This surge of reflective activity, new policy development, and rationalisation and integration of existing policies and programmes at national levels follows on current perceptions of the nature and magnitude of the economic, social and environmental problems that are emerging from post-war trends of urbanisation.

From the standpoint of urban growth, the economic policy concerns are reflected in the different levels, mixes and rates of growth of economic activity found in cities or urban areas of different size and location. The shares of activity in faster and slower growing industrial sectors, in higher or lower productivity (and therefore, higher or lower wage paying) industries, with diversified or mono-skilled and trained occupational structures, and in polluting or clean industries, differ greatly between the many urban areas and different countries. Based on the experience of reinforcement of such divergencies between locales in the private sectors of free enterprise economies, it is difficult to imagine amelioration of these kinds of imbalances in the absence of the application of relevant urban growth polices aimed at redistributing future and perhaps present economic activity locations.

Social policy concerns in urban growth manifest themselves as concentrations of population with either relatively high or low incomes, with high or low educational or training status, with majority or minority ethnic or racial characteristics, and, given any of the above attributes, with relatively good or poor physical accessibility to such a reasonable array of goods, services and environmental amenities as is expected to be available in the given social milieu. For policy purposes, some of these social concerns are closely associated with economic opportunity changes in a given urban locale and, thereby, respond to a common set of instruments applied to economic ends. But a number of them respond to general and specific redistributions of goods, services and environmental amenities in the public sector; for example, educational and training facilities, health and medical establishments and clinics, open space and recreational facilities, and the like. The latter are probably best viewed as social redistribu-

3

tional elements not primarily concerned with raising or maintaining industrial efficiency or job and private income growth in an urban area, especially in the short run.

Finally, the concerns of physical environmental quality in urban growth present themselves in the forms of concentrations or dispersals of polluting industries, in congestion of people and activities as represented by higher-than-desirable living and working densities and extreme impedences of goods and people movements within and between urban areas, and in over- or under-representation of physical amenities in both the built and natural environments in different urban areas, each having their own unique man-made urban and nature-provided ecological heritages. The interactions between urban growth policies and those policies aimed at developing or protecting environmental amenities in present and future man-built or natural areas in advanced countries are critical because the environmental potentials created and burdens imposed are tightly interwoven with the location, composition, and pace of growth of population and activities in particular geographical locales.

As is the usual practise, these common policy concerns have been defined, so far, in terms of the problematic and negative aspects of urban growth and change and not in terms of its positive attributes. Normally, one could say that if it is not a problem it is not a policy concern. While there is truth in this statement, we must recognise that certain of the positive or beneficial aspects of urban growth need to be capitalised on and reinforced through public policies in order to eliminate or vitiate the more severe problems associated with such growth. For this reason, we must take into specific account the benefits of scale economies and externalities created through certain levels of population and activity concentration and interactions between particular mixes of private and public sector functions or entities. In a strict benefit-cost framework, one would desire to balance the total levels of economies and diseconomies generated by urban areas of any given size by guiding their growth to sizes at which the rates of change in each of these former phenomena were equal, thereby maximising the net economies or benefits being generated.

We make no pretence of engaging in such a balancing act in this evaluation. Nonetheless, the more serious implications for policy implementation that arise from ignoring either the required threshold levels of size and composition of activity or the possible redundancies in overall size and sectoral representation are evaluated in our subsequent selected discussions of instrument application experience. The implications are measured by, for example, changes in relative levels and rates of: (a) overall population and activity growth; (b) major structural shifts among population and activity components; and (c) available indices of efficiency or welfare change such as income, value added by economic enterprises, product and service outputs and costs in private and public sectors, types and densities of major land-use configurations, and relative physical and spatial accessibility or exposure to environmental amenities or deficiences in and between urban areas.

These common policy concerns comprise what is felt to be a sufficiently comprehensive context for purposes of evaluating the effectiveness and effects of urban growth policy instrument applications in our selected Western European and North American countries during the post-Second World War period. Virtually all of them fall within the scope of the social concerns outlined in the recent OECD publication that is intended to lay the basis for longer-term development of social indicators for use by these countries.[1]

The need for evaluation of national policies of urban growth and the instruments for their implementation arises as much from the need to define the nature and role of such policies as from the need to judge their specific effectiveness. The explicit mention of urban growth policies at the national level of concern is a fairly recent phenomenon in most of these countries. There has been a plethora of 'urban policies' in the past, to be sure. These have dealt with a vast array of specific socio-economic and physical development problems: urban renewal to combat inner city decay; open space land to humanise the man-built landscape with natural amenity; myriad social programmes to alleviate human dislocations in the larger, older cities; and new town or community programmes that have attempted larger scale socio-economic and physical structuring and rationalisation in potential new growth locales, mostly on the fringes of larger expanding urban agglomerations.

The fallacy of composition, or the 'adding-up problem', would keep one from claiming that all of these separate efforts sum up to a national set of urban growth policies. Past results indicate that the whole is indeed less than the sum of the parts. Urban policies that have focused on restructuring certain troublesome elements observed in the overall trends of urbanisation have had little evident effect on the magnitude or direction of those trends. This is not unfairly to criticise the results obtained from specific efforts such as renewal or new towns. They have often been quite successful when judged in their own frames of reference. It is just to say that they do not together constitute a set of national policies that has kept the largest urban agglomerations from becoming massive and congested, nor have they materially assisted in creating major alternatives for balanced urban growth elsewhere in cities or urban areas of more moderate size.

The logical question at this point is, of course, precisely what do previous urban policies fail to add up to? The broad menu of policy concerns already presented reflects the enormous complexity of this general area of policy relating to urban growth and development. Because of this complex nature, we could envision work on the subject being divided into the two main categories of 'growth' and 'form and structure of development'. According to traditional definitions in the physical and social sciences, growth implies mainly quantitative changes in size of the phenomena or entities under observation, while development infers qualitative change involving structural alteration in the relationships of their constituent parts to one another.

This study of urban growth policy clearly intends to focus on the actions taken to change or maintain the size of different urban areas as measured by the levels and rates of change in total population and activity within and between defined geographic entities. In contrast, work on selected detailed aspects of form and structure problems in urban areas would relate largely to the special kinds of previously used urban policies and instruments referred to above that have been designed to deal with particular qualitative dimensions of urbanisation and do not claim to address issues arising from the need to promote or control change with respect to the sizes of urban areas as such.[2]

While it is neither possible nor necessary here to delve into the implementation of policies dealing with the various detailed problems of urban area form and structure, the analysis and evaluation of growth policy must identify and deal with the strategic structural components and qualitative dimensions of urban change. The questions of which are the key population groups, private industry sectors, and public functions and activities that are the prime agents producing faster or slower growth, and in what combination, must be addressed. Likewise, the questions of what mix or mixes of people and private and public activities must be present in urban areas to produce 'balanced growth', i.e. the desired combinations of the economic, social, and physical environmental attributes of an urban area, in order to fulfil the necessary and sufficient conditions defined in national policy objectives, have to be faced.

The fatal problem in attempting to provide neat and systematic evaluation according to a well-defined set of criteria for urban growth policy, especially across several national experiences, is simply that virtually none of the selected countries have in existence or operation a single comprehensive legislative authority, or even an integrated set of such authorities, covering urban growth policy and specifying the range of policy concerns outlined above in the form of operating objectives and guidelines for implementation. What do exist in most of these countries are complicated patterns of rationalisation of existing policies and programmes, legislative and executive pronouncements of concern, and proposed legislation that is progressively offering an identifiable and more consistent basis for the establishment and implementation of something that could be called national policies for urban growth. It is on the basis of this latter pragmatic process of piecemeal and fractionated articulation of the nature and objective of national urban growth policy taking place in the selected countries more active in this field that our analysis and evaluation are fashioned.[3]

Even though there do not yet exist, in most of these countries, formal national urban growth policies and programmes with their own histories of experience, it is vital to define the relationship of the incipient efforts to guide and foster urban growth to other established growth policies and programmes, i.e. national programmes of regional development, environmental quality, and land-use planning. This is because these different policies and programmes often use the same instruments of implementation, but either to different (compatible or conflicting) ends or to common ends with different (effective or ineffective) methods of application. As the processes of policy and programme restructuring proceed in our study countries, there is a likelihood that major instruments of policy will be regrouped under newer and differently-defined sets of policies, i.e. aimed at different objectives and employed more effectively than in the past.

Notes

[1] OECD, Manpower and Social Affairs Directorate, *List of Social Concerns Common to Most OECD Countries*, OECD, Paris 1973.
[2] Examples of specific subjects relating to the form and structure of urban development might be found in such areas as those that deal with, for example, problems of urban sprawl or continuous spatial extension of urban areas; rehabilitation of the older, declining portions within urban areas and their services; public land ownership as a tool to facilitate development; and the effects of land market controls and interventions on the location, pace, and distribution of burdens and benefits arising from development within urban areas.
[3] Government documents and publications, the independent expert literature, and personal consultations and discussions by the author directly

with government and professional experts in the respective countries under study provide the basis for both the country's specific and the more generalised descriptions of policy and statements of objectives. Sources specific to a particular country and its policies are referenced in the section(s) dealing with that country. Generalised policy descriptions and statements of objectives are made at the lowest possible level of generality and abstraction while remaining substantially inclusive of the experience of all of the countries under consideration.

2   Purpose and Structure of the Study

Our primary aim is to identify the instruments available and being used to implement policies of urban growth and distribution, to judge the effectiveness and related effects of their use, and to evaluate the extent of current and potential future innovation. Substantively, this means treating the twin sets of policies guiding applications of instruments to control or to moderate growth and size in the largest and densest urban agglomerations and to stimulate growth and elevate size and, perhaps, density, in the smaller and medium-sized urban areas. It is the overarching set of issues spanning simultaneous pursuit of these twin sets of policies at the national level that is our primary concern. Therefore, the operational objectives. actual trends of growth, implementation strategies, and effectiveness and effects of instrument use across the previously enumerated areas of policy concern must be defined and their consequences evaluated in tandem for the largest and for the moderately-sized centres of urban growth. Our study will focus on the problems of co-ordination and the dilemmas of consistent policy execution at the national level when explicit or implicit attempts are made (or not made) to carry out a strategy linking urban growth constraint in large agglomerations with urban growth stimulation in alternative centres of opportunity.[1]

The trend in some countries, as evidenced in our subsequent case examples of policy innovation, towards integrating the traditional regional growth and urban form and structure policies, seems to be based on a growing awareness that neither of these kinds of policy is effective when implemented in isolation from the other. To combat problems of low income and high unemployment in under-industrialised or economically obsolescent regions directly by merely subsidising manufacturing plant locations randomly across a large geographic landscape has been proved unsatisfactory from a number of viewpoints, social and environmental as well as economic. This dissatisfaction has been borne out by recent evaluations of the Appalachian and other regional experience in the United States,[2] the Northland stimulation effort in Sweden,[3] the regional action and related programmes in the Federal Republic of Germany,[4] regional policies in The Netherlands,[5] and regional economic policies in France.[6]

These types of direct attack on specific economic problems ignore the necessary conditions that must be brought into existence for self-sustaining economic growth and social modernisation or revitalisation to begin to emerge in a region, i.e. the thresholds that need to be attained either simultaneously or sequentially in the private and public sectors to create the positive externalities or agglomerative effects that generate industrial efficiency and personal opportunity.

On the other hand, to struggle with the problems of physical congestion and pollution, social disorganisation, and other forms of functional obsolescence in the existing large urbanised agglomerations with no thought of the ultimate absorptive capacity of such areas, is to invite equal frustration with urban policies as with regional ones. This linkage of the problems of revitalising and restructuring the large urban agglomeration with those of generating growth in alternative areas is probably best exemplified by British experience in controlling the growth of London while simultaneously stimulating growth in the development areas and in some of the more recently designated new towns that are intended to serve as larger centres of growth outside of the existing agglomerations. The effects of such policy for London have not been without problems, as we shall see, but should be instructive nonetheless for countries such as the United States where disappointment has become widespread among those who had unrealistically high expectations for urban renewal and the myriad 'war on poverty' programmes to solve most, if not all, of the problems of massive agglomerations such as the New York Consolidated Metropolitan Area.

This trend toward operationally linking policies for creating viable centres of balanced growth in newer or smaller urban areas with those for reconversion of older or larger urban areas is of strategic importance in shaping feasible and effective national policies of urban growth and relating them to traditional urban policies dealing with form and structure. Reconversion problems will always be with us, since all cities, of whatever size, eventually grow older and progressively more obsolete for many aspects of living. The tractability of problem solution or amelioration is the question at issue; i.e. the socio-economic cost and political/institutional manageability of reconversion efforts may be easily tractable in a city of half a million people, higher but within feasible range in a metropolitan area of a million or so people, but astronomical and beyond control in a massive agglomeration of ten to fifteen million people.

The section of our study dealing with models and analyses selects, from among the competing normative and positive hypotheses explaining growth processes and outcome, the most relevant and believable ones that are capable of providing a reasonably unified theme for judging the validity and value of the emerging urban growth policy implementation experiences in particular countries. This is done in the light of the kinds of policy concerns enunciated earlier and with respect to the major kinds of implementation problems. The hypotheses and arguments developed for our purposes largely deal with:

(1) the key private and public sectors (industries and functional groupings) and decision-making units that provide the leverage points for public intervention to affect growth and distribution in beneficial ways;
(2) the political and managerial arrangements that produce the functionally/sectorally co-ordinated and spatially/temporally consistent application of bundles of individual policy instruments in a synergistic fashion; and
(3) the different normative schemas for evaluating results within and between the various national experiences.

In the later section on policy instruments available for use, we identify the basic policy 'tool kit' that is present in essentially all of our mixed economy study countries. These instruments, in the way they are defined, constitute the raw material for policy implementation, but may be fashioned and combined with one another in an infinite variety of ways. In practice, of course, we find that there is a large but finite number of ways in which the instruments are used. The main variations of the theme of urban growth policy implementation are exemplified by the experience and innovation occurring at national levels in these countries.

While scrutiny of actual use experience in individual countries is essential because of the diversities in socio-cultural contexts, governmental and institutional arrangements, and histories of policy development and specific problems faced at a given time, our concluding perspective attempts to draw back together some of these diverse strands to offer conclusions on both important particularistic results obtained and any definite patterns of commonality or lead and lag relationships in instrument application between countries. We then sift from these assessments our recommendations for continued innovation in the use of policy instruments in the future.

Notes

[1] Examples of growth control policies for agglomerations are confined to European experience, e.g., London, Paris, and the Randstad, Holland. Smaller centres for urban growth promotion can be found in the experience of both American and European countries, e.g., St John's NB, Canada: Cordoba, Spain; Regensberg, West Germany; Irvine, Scotland, UK; Lulea, Sweden; and Groningen, The Netherlands.

[2] Niles M. Hansen, 'Regional policy in the United States', mimeo, University of Texas, Austin, Texas, 1973.

[3] Åke E. Andersson, 'Regional economic policy – the Swedish experience', mimeo, Göteborg Economic Institute, March 1973.

[4] Günter Krumme, 'Regional policies in West Germany', mimeo, Department of Geography, University of Washington, Seattle 1973.

[5] Ad. J. Hendriks and S. Panitchpakdi, 'Regional policy in the Netherlands', mimeo, Netherlands Economic Institute, Erasmus University, Rotterdam, March 1973.

[6] Rémy Prud'homme, 'Regional economic policy in France, 1962–1972', mimeo, BETURE, Paris, March 1973.

PART II

Models and Analyses to Guide Policy Application

3 The Objects of Policy: Working Definitions of Urban Areas and Growth Sectors

The geographic entities and the private and public sectors and dimensions of growth and change need a definition rooted in the realities of actual experience which, at the same time, provides operational usefulness for the effective application of the instruments of policy. Such definitions as are presently employed for the purposes of policy implementation dealing with both urban and non-urban population and activity growth and distribution between areas and regions of a country are, at best, only partially relevant for addressing the policy concerns expressed in the first part of this book. The geographic areas, sectors of activity, and qualitative dimensions of change that have been defined for purposes of implementing the traditional regional and physical environmental policies require definitional revision and extension.

For example, areal definition under regional economic policies is typically based on identifying sizeable geographic regions with a fairly narrow range of common negative or problem attributes, e.g. low income, high unemployment, or low productivity. Looking at the designated Assisted Areas of Great Britain in Figure 3.1, we can see that sizeable proportions of the national territory containing a variety of cities or urban areas and physical landscapes are included. The Special Development Areas, with greater problem severity and higher levels of assistance, do tend to be clustered around some of the larger urban agglomerations, i.e. Glasgow and Newcastle. The Intermediate Areas, with lesser problem severity and lower levels of assistance, and the totally unassisted area encompass a number of other large urban centres, e.g. Cardiff, Bristol, Plymouth and Birmingham. From this classification, based on the degree of the economic problem experienced, however, one can infer little or nothing about the potential for or direction and nature of growth likely to occur in any urban area of the country. The following areal and sectoral definitions attempt to discriminate in such a way as to reveal the nature and direction of the spatial incidence of population and activity, and their beneficial and problem attributes as produced by public and private decision-making entities.

15

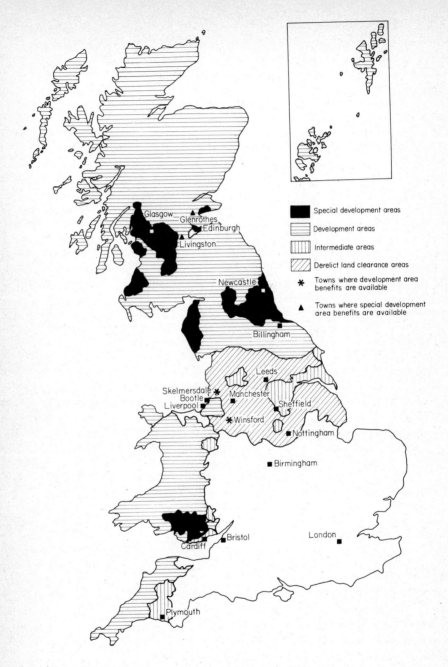

Fig. 3.1   The Assisted Areas in Great Britain, 1972.

Source: Secretary of State for Trade and Industry, *Industrial and Regional Development*, HMSO, London, March 1972, p. 12.

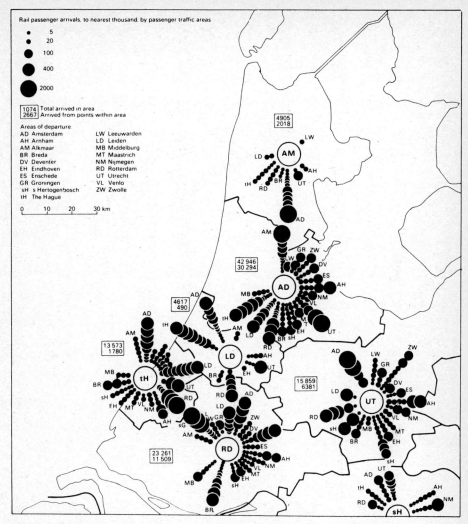

Fig. 3.2   Passenger commuter traffic by rail in the Randstad, 1959.

Note: Time by intercity trains between main Randstad centres:

Amsterdam–Haarlem	13 minutes
Amsterdam–The Hague	41 minutes
Amsterdam–Utrecht	25 minutes
Amsterdam–Utrecht	31 minutes
Rotterdam–Amsterdam	58 minutes
Rotterdam–Utrecht	34 minutes

Source: T. R. P. Lawrence, *Randstad, Holland,* Oxford University Press, London 1973, p. 36.

Area definition for urban policy analysis

For our purposes, urban areas are defined on a two-fold basis. Primarily, they are defined as daily living and job market areas, which means that: (a) they constitute the geographic locale within which the active population of job seekers can obtain employment without having to change residence and within which most daily and other shorter-term social, cultural and physical amenities are sought and enjoyed; and (b) they constitute the physical daily commuting shed from periphery to centre(s), with the outer geographic boundary being the one that connects those points or districts beyond which an insignificant proportion of people are commuting to the dominant centre, say, less than 5 or 10 per cent. This definition deals with an inward flowing phenomenon and its measures are indices of the centripetal force exerted by powerful cities on their surrounding regions.

In mono centric agglomerations, such as Paris, the dominant commuter flows may be clearly converging at a central area in the region. The polycentric agglomerations, such as the Randstad and the Rhine–Ruhr, make clear-cut areal definition more difficult. There are obvious dominant centres of influence in each of these latter agglomerations, but closure of their respective labour markets does not exist and there is much cross-commuting. This is illustrated by Figure 3.2, in which it is seen that residents in each of the major Randstad centres are commuting widely among all the other centres, as well as to their own. It remains a matter of some judgement as to what degree of closure is required to define separate areas, but our working assumption is that cross-commuting on roughly the Randstad level should be occurring for a polycentric urban region to be considered a single functional agglomeration from the residence/job opportunity linkage viewpoint.

Secondarily, urban areas are defined as centres of service and influence over geographic hinterlands of varying size. In this sense they constitute the geographic locales within which the external economies and diseconomies generated by the agglomeration of activities on varying scales are experienced. To a great extent this definition deals with an outward flowing phenomenon and its measures are indices of the centrifugal force exerted for urban expansion as clusters of activity decentralise from relatively more concentrated centres.

This means that areas are defined on the basis of the geographic range of goods, services, and communications provided by private and public organisations clustered within the region, but progressively spreading out from the core or centre without breaking their linkages with the dominant activities in that core or centre. Measures of such linkages are provided by daily newspaper circulation areas, wholesale storage and delivery networks, banking and financial service provision areas, telephone service areas including toll-free zones, and retail trading areas.

In Figure 3.3, we can see an estimate of spheres of influence of French cities based on such measures, in addition to job commuting patterns. The solid line denoting 'zone of commercial influence' refers to '... the undisputed shopping and business area of the city'.[1] This geographical area often coincides approximately with the daily commuting shed of the centre and thereby provides a dual-based definition of an urban area for the daily routine and ubiquitous types of functions, i.e. Berry's 'daily urban system'. The potential congruence of service and commuting areas is illustrated by Figures 3.4 and 3.5 where these two types of areal defini-

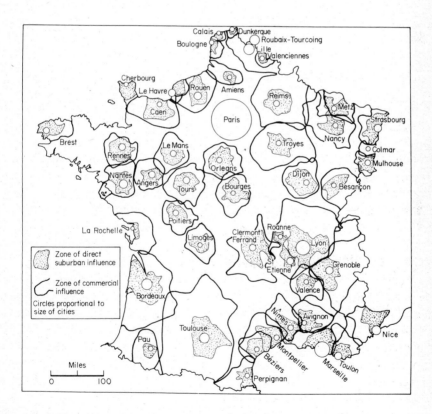

Fig. 3.3   Spheres of influence of cities in France.

Source: Robert E. Dickenson, *The City Region in Western Europe,* Rourledge and Kegan Paul Ltd., London 1967, p. 147.

19

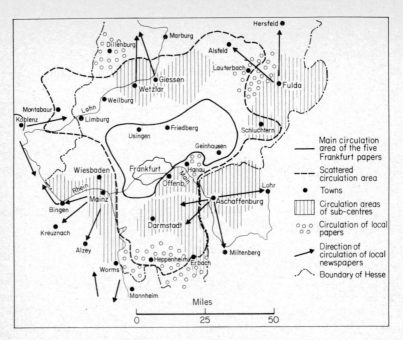

Fig. 3.4   The city-region of Frankfurt: newspaper circulations of the central places.

Source: Dickenson, op. cit., pp. 155 and 156.

tion are mapped for Frankfurt. The dotted line in Figure 3.4 of scattered circulation for Frankfurt newspapers approximates the contour traced by the beaded line in Figure 3.5 of the outer limit of commuting to the centre of Frankfurt.

Dickenson explains that there are two further lines demarcating influences that are not mapped in Figure 3.3, i.e. an 'economic curve' which is measured by the outer limit of the commercial and banking relations that embrace all other local functions, and a 'cultural curve' which is measured by the range of leading university and newspaper influence. Here the role of Paris as financier, educator, and editorialist for the nation is well known.

In terms of outward-spreading influence, then, there is a major set of activities in an urban centre that generates externalities or mutual interdependencies through spatial clustering for the immediate surrounding hinterland largely coincident with the commuting shed. This defines a geographical entity, from and to which people and activities migrate for living and working, that can serve as the object of urban growth policy. Further,

20

there is another major set of activities in large metropolitan centres that exerts influence and generates externalities through linkages to private and public enterprises across entire nations or large regions that extend far beyond their commuting sheds. These latter national and international urban functions may be largely concentrated in a single city in some countries, e.g. entertainment, cultural, governmental and financial functions in London, Paris, Stockholm and the Randstad; or dispersed among several cities with a division of labour in some countries, e.g. cultural, entertainment and financial functions in New York, government in Washington, DC, and cultural/educational in Boston, for the United States. The only policy-relevant observation offered on these phenomena at this point is that, while urban agglomerations are required to support great clusterings of nation-servicing functions, there apparently is no locational

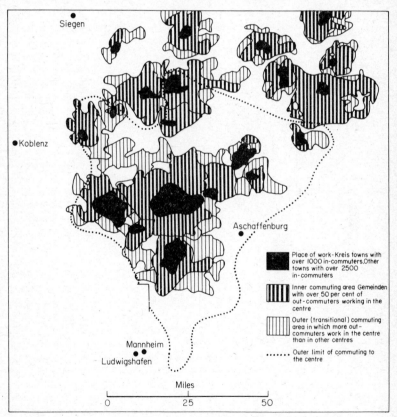

Fig. 3.5 The city-region of Frankfurt: commuting to selected cities in Hesse, 1950.

Source: Dickenson, op. cit., pp. 155 and 156.

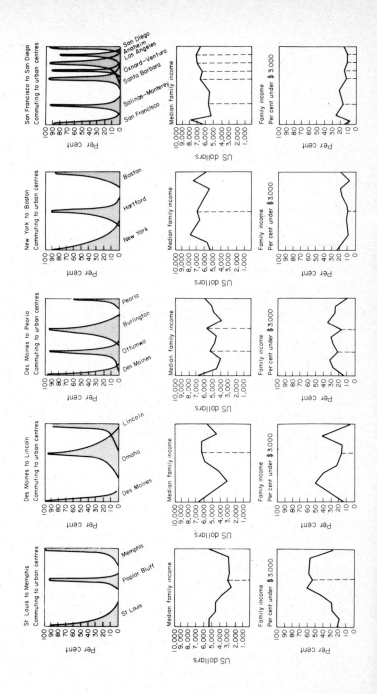

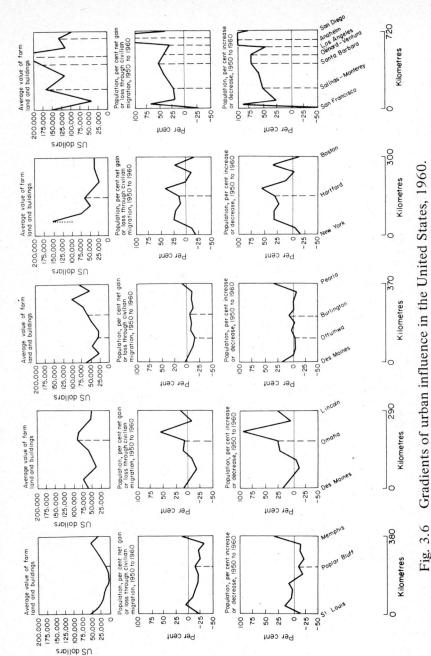

Fig. 3.6   Gradients of urban influence in the United States, 1960.

Source: B. J. L. Berry, 'The geography of the United States in the year 2000' *Transactions of British Geographers* no. 51, November 1970, pp. 30 and 31.

23

imperative for an 'over-concentration' of all such activities in a single metropolitan area.

For purposes of urban growth and distribution policy evaluation, we can recognise that urban entities still tend to organise themselves around relatively high density foci of activity and to produce significant benefits for their resident populations, and, perhaps, significant costs after a certain degree of concentration is attained. These urban spatial organisations can be identified and related to policy action even in the context of the otherwise physically undifferentiated field of urbanisation produced by the coalescence of built-up landscape in the megalopolis.

On the other hand, we can take account of the fact, as suggested by the analysis of Berry,[2] that the greatest future growth potential exists for those urban areas that are least isolated from the existing large fields of externality influence. The enormous accumulation of social and economic overhead capital in the form of private activity clusters, transport and communication networks, and public service institutions conveys great relative growth advantage on the nearest physically discrete and outlying urban areas from the great inner concentrations of London, Paris, and New York. As the largest agglomerations expand outward, new and functionally differentiated outlying urban areas emerge on a relatively large scale. Rather than remaining physically discrete, their commuting sheds overlap with that of the older dominant centre and the built environment becomes continuous between such areas.

The relationships between the commuting sheds of different functional urban areas, both in megalopolitan contexts where much overlap exists and for independent situations with gaps between commuting periphery, are graphed for the transverses between selected major metropolitan centres in the United States in Figure 3.6. The columns of charts under each transverse illustrate key growth and welfare variables associated positively (except for a percentage of poverty families) with the rising and falling commuting sheds graphed in the top row of charts. The transverse from St Louis to Memphis of some 380 kilometres shows complete separation between the respective commuting sheds with the implication that growth could still be promoted at an intermediate location, i.e. Poplar Bluff, to retain physical separation of these urban areas. The transverse from Santa Barbara to San Diego of a roughly comparable distance, on the other hand, reveals five overlapping commuter sheds implying existing continuous urbanisation with virtually no opportunity for growth promotion of physically separate urban areas along this coastal megalopolis.

One important aspect of the following policy instrument evaluations is the question of the feasibility and desirability of such alternative courses of action as:

24

(1)   creating and maintaining a physical hiatus in the built environment on the model of London's Green Belt and new and expanding towns with a view to displacing growth outward in the South East region to other independent urban areas from the job/residence linkage viewpoint; and
(2)   promoting balanced growth of independent urban areas entirely outside the present conurbations where some economic export base exists but where conurbation externalities cannot be drawn on or where the influence of the latter is relatively weak.

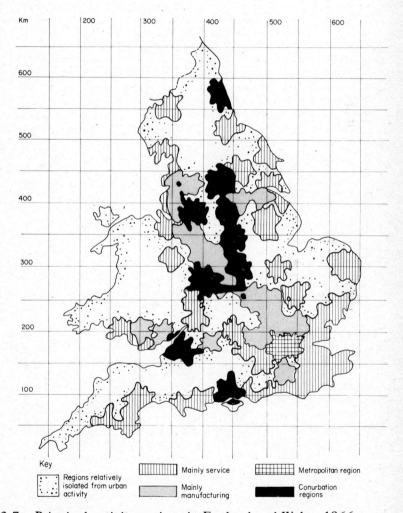

Fig. 3.7   Principal activity regions in England and Wales, 1966.

Source: Garbis Armen, 'A classification of cities and city regions in England and Wales, 1966' *Regional Studies* vol. 6, no. 2, June 1972, p. 178.

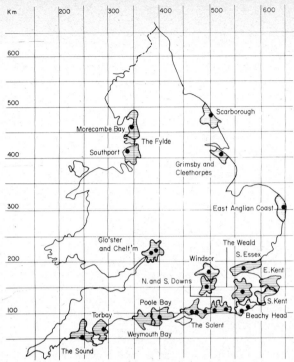

Fig. 3.8 Holiday/retirement regions in England and Wales.

Source: Armen, op. cit., p. 175.

Examples of this kind of choice are present in virtually every country under study in light of persistent growth distribution trends, e.g. the rapid growth rates of the rings of cities just beyond the commuting sheds of Paris, London or the Randstad. In contrast to our map of the Assisted Areas (Fig. 3.1), the areal definition presented in Figure 3.7 lends itself more directly to formulating decisions on choices for growth policy. The mapping of England and Wales is now organised around areas of growth or non-growth, areas of urban coalescence producing megalopolitan regions, and areas dominated by major sectoral characteristics such as service or manufacturing activity. Since what we call urban growth constitutes many variations on a theme, we can move along this definitional path to evaluate specialised forms of growth potential responding to shifting or restructured societal demands and production possibilities, as illustrated by the respective mappings of emerging holiday and retirement centres in Figure 3.8 and administrative and market centres in Figure 3.9. Even in the small and constrained space of Britain, it is apparent how the holiday/retirement locales hug the seashore and rely on maintenance of natural

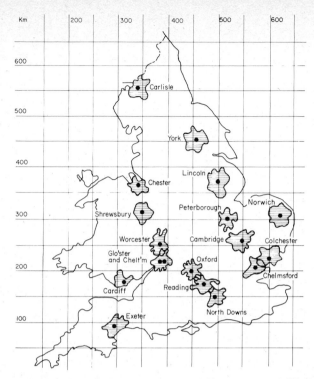

Fig. 3.9   Administrative/market regions in England and Wales.
Source: Armen, op. cit., p. 175.

environmental amenities, while the administrative/market locales flank the
great central conurbation strip to feed off its externalities and yet simultaneously try to provide better than average residential amenity to more
discriminating workers and households.

Recent criticism of conventional definitions of urban areas, especially
those that approximate the SMSA (Standard Metropolitan Statistical
Area) as used in the United States, centre on the argument that vast fields
of urbanisation are emerging that will swamp traditional urban spatial
structure. We can accept some aspects of this argument and recognise that
the scale of urban areas, as measured by population and physical area, has
been increasing steadily for as far back as we can obtain comparative
statistics. Table 3.1 shows that, during the twentieth century, the average
size of metropolitan areas in the United States has increased by anywhere
from one-third to four times their populations in 1900. The physical
expansion of Stockholm is graphically charted for the past century in
Figure 3.10. While we can agree that scale has risen, we need not necessari-
ly capitulate to the assertion that 'urban fields' are inevitably coming

27

Table 3.1

Average size of United States metropolitan areas,
by region, 1900 and 1960

	1900	1960	1960/1900
New England	375,307	597,787	1·59
Middle Atlantic	603,140	1,188,806	1·97
East North Central	391,957	578,432	1·48
West North Central	283,371	370,322	1·31
South Atlantic	216,713	396,022	1·83
East South Central	219,881	310,281	1·41
West South Central	188,439	292,349	1·55
Mountain	130,796	257,551	1·97
Pacific	254,418	1,085,516	4·27

Source: Benjamin Chinitz and Richard Dusansky, 'Patterns of urbanization within regions of the United States' *Urban Studies* vol. 9, no. 3, October 1972, p. 293.

which will demand megalopolitan-sized regions to contain them.

Spatial organisation for growth appears to be occurring at sub-megalopolitan scales, much as we have defined it. There are examples of urban areas, such as Stockholm, which, because of historical good fortune, have grown but maintained a physical separation from other urban areas and a high accessibility to natural amenity and non-urban environment. Much of this kind of advantage has been lost to urban areas of similar size that are buried in the North-east Megalopolis of the United States.

Some of this kind of advantage has been salvaged, however, for London through intervention and assertion of the public will to reorient the direction and locale of future urban growth in Great Britain away from the threatening urban field in the South-East. There at least seems to be the possibility of positive public intervention into urban growth to maintain a manageable scale in diverse locations, as discussed in the following section on growth trends.

In most of our study countries, the metropolitan areas that are defined for statistical purposes tend to be 'underbounded' in relation to our definition of urban area. But these data-gathering boundaries are continually being extended to account for increasing sizes of urban areas. The movement outward from the centres of older cities or urban areas with more

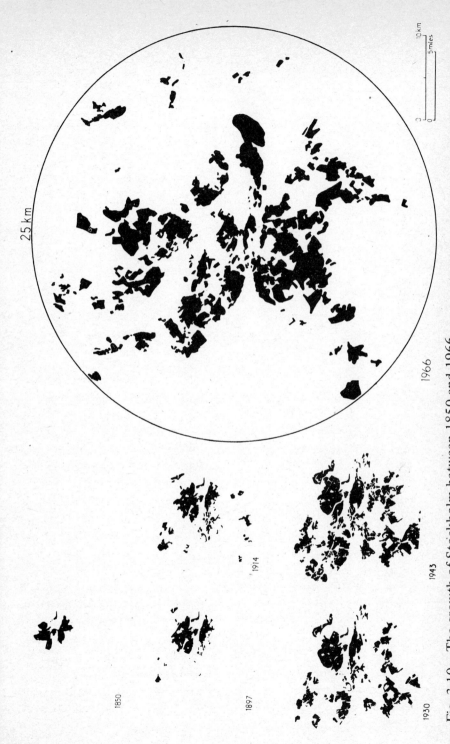

25 km

1966

10 km
5 miles

0

Fig. 3.10   The growth of Stockholm between 1850 and 1966.
Source: Ella Ödmann and Gun-Butt Dahlberg, *Urbanization in Sweden,* Government Publishing, Stockholm.

1850

1897

1914

1930

1943

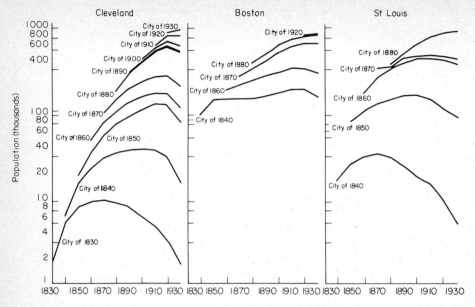

Fig. 3.11   Population of three major US cities at different dates, according to different city boundaries.

Source: Marion Clawson, *Suburban Land Conversion in the United States,* 2, The John Hopkins Press, Baltimore 1971, p. 34.

extensive settlement patterns resulting from rising incomes and technological changes necessitates redefinition as indicated in Figure 3.11. While some observers claim that central city decline and suburban growth are post-war phenomena in the United States, we can see that the under-bounded cities of an earlier age, the Cleveland of 1830 for example, lost their relevance as comprehensive definitions for the centres and surrounding hinterlands of their urban areas before the end of the nineteenth century.

But again we can remind ourselves that, in spite of increasing size, there are still options open to decide where growth should occur and of what degree and kind. The actual proportions of land from national totals that are used for urban-built environment and its immediate influences are miniscule. The leverage in terms of land area for accommodating population and generating socio-economic benefits is enormous – about 20 to 1 in the case of the North-east Megalopolis – as illustrated in Figure 3.12. On something less than 1 per cent of the United States' land area, we find that of the order of 20 per cent of the national population, workers, and personal income have been generated.

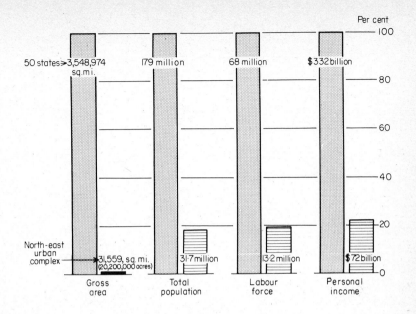

Fig. 3.12 North-eastern urban complex in relation to the whole United States, 1960.

Source: Clawson, op. cit., p. 197.

Growth sectors: the urban shift to quaternary functions and geographic centrality

In turning to the sectoral and functional definitions of urban growth, perhaps the best place to begin is with Gottmann's definitional extensions of modern private and public activities to what he calls the quaternary sector. In explaining the concept of quaternary functions and in defining the content of this sector of activity, Gottmann emphasises the demand and need for centrality with relatively large clusterings of productive activities in the central portions of urban areas. Definitionally, the quaternary sector is:

> dominated by transactions and by executive, legislative, judicial, and commercial functions. However, two new categories of academic work and research have to be added to the constellation of activities generating urban centrality.... The old classification of occupations and economic activities in three sectors ... the primary producing raw materials; the secondary, processing them into finished goods; the tertiary, consisting of services, ... is no longer adequate. We must

31

Table 3.2

Percentage distribution of gross domestic product, 1951–52 and 1961–62
(percentage shares of gross domestic product costs)

Country	Agriculture		Industry		Construction		Services	
	1951–52	1961–62	1951–52	1961–62	1951–52	1961–62	1951–52	1961–62
France	13	9	43	41	6	7	39	43
West Germany	10	5	46	46	5	7	39	41
Netherlands	14	9	34	42	6	–	47	48
United Kingdom	6	4	41	41	5	7	48	49
Combined average of above countries	12	8	41	40	6	7	42	44
United States	7	4	34	32	5	5	54	59

Note: 1951–52 at current prices, 1961–62 at current prices.
Source: Secretariat, Economic Commission for Europe, *Economic Survey of Europe in 1965*, Part I, 'The European economy in 1963', Chapter II, p. 23.

Table 3.3

Changes in office and other workers in employment by industry group,
England and Wales, 1951–61

	Total		Office workers		Others		Office workers as percentage of total	
	thousands	%	thousands	%	thousands	%	1951	1961
Total	1,419	7	1,118	40	301	2	15	19
Extractive	−342	−20	20	57	−362	−22	2	4
Manufacturing	407	6	367	40	40	1	12	17
Construction	189	15	53	73	136	12	6	9
Services	1,088	12	665	37	423	6	20	24

Source: EFTA, 'Towards national urban development strategies', Economic Development Committee, Working Party on New Patterns of Settlement, Geneva, September 1972, no page number.

Table 3.4

Growth in managerial and clerical employment in England and Wales, 1961–66

Occupations	1961 (thousands)	1966 (thousands)	Changes 1961–66 (thousands)	%
All occupations	21,694	22,896	1,202	*5·5*
Office workers	4,438	5,089	651	*14·7*
Administrative and professional	1,465	1,767	302	20·6
Clerical	2,973	3,323	350	11·8

Source: EFTA, op. cit., no page number.

recognise a quaternary sector of economic activities corresponding to the transactional work which now employs managerial, professional and higher-level technical personnel.[3]

Our main purpose, then, in growth sector classification, is to focus on occupational structure, which emphasises job distinctions and attributes such as: office versus factory work; high status versus low status; educational requirements and sophistication of the work; income and responsibility advancement potential; and the productivity or efficiency gains or losses associated with relatively more rapid expansion of jobs in the tertiary and quaternary sectors.

The moderately heavier reliance of growth in output on the service sector (defined here primarily as the tertiary sector) in some of our study countries during the 1950s is shown in Table 3.2 by the changes in percentage shares of output for the different sectors. These estimates of changing shares of service activity probably underestimate the growth of service jobs because many work positions are shifting from manufacturing plants to offices, especially for highly skilled quaternary functions in high technology industries.

There is an indication that such employment shifts have been important in restructuring employment opportunities in countries, as exemplified by the changes seen in Tables 3.3 and 3.4 for England and Wales and in Tables 3.5 and 3.6 for Sweden. All industry sectors in England and Wales have experienced several times the rate of growth in office jobs as they have in traditional farm hand and assembly line positions. Further, a greater rate of growth has been experienced in administrative and professional jobs than in clerical positions. In Sweden as well, job growth

Table 3.5

Production and employment by type of economic activity in the period 1961–70

Type of activity	Change in employment (%) per five-year period		Change in production (%) per five-year period (volume)	
	1961–1965	1966–1970	1961–1965	1965–1970
Agriculture and forestry	−23·4	−23·9	− 0·5	+ 2·5
Mining and manufacturing	+ 4·2	− 2·7	+46·9	+30·7
Building and construction	+17·2	+ 1·9	+41·6	+ 9·9
Commercial services	+ 4·6	+ 3·7	+27·6	+20·5
Public services	+26·9	+33·4	+19·3	+25·2
Total	+ 3·7	+ 2·8	+33·2	+23·4

Source: Swedish Ministry of Labour and Housing, 'Report on regional policy in Sweden', mimeo, 2 March 1973, p. 12.

Table 3.6

Employment in different branches of services in the period 1961–70

Branch	No. employed			Percentage change	
	1960	1965	1970	1961–1965	1966–1970
Trade	478,000	534,000	534,000	+11·7	+ 0·0
Transport	242,000	247,000	251,000	+ 2·1	+ 1·6
Public services	393,000	503,000	696,000	+27·9	+38·3
Consultant services	34,000	60,000	81,000	+76·4	+35·0
Other services	271,000	251,000	279,000	− 8·3	+10·0
Total	1,418,000	1,595,000	1,841,000	+13·2	+15·4

Source: Swedish Ministry of Labour and Housing, ibid., p. 15.

has been much faster in consultant and public services than in the traditional trade and commercial services.

This transformation of the more rapid sectoral growth from the secondary to the tertiary and quaternary sectors provides two basic sets of issues in the application of policy instruments aimed at promoting or controlling urban growth with which a number of national governments are now grappling. First, there is the change in occupational structure itself towards jobs requiring progressively more education, training, and technical and intellectual sophistication. Associated with this change are shifts to more discriminating tastes with respect to social, cultural and physical environmental amenities. These preferences are translated into effective demand for such goods and services through rising real incomes and greater proportions of leisure time.

Table 3.7

Employment structure (percentages) of Greater London, South East Standard Region and England and Wales, 1951 to 1969 by workplace

	Primary	Manufacturing	Construction	Services
*Greater London**				
1951	0·5	33·3	6·5	59·7
1961	0·3	33·1	6·2	60·4
1966	0·3	30·5	6·3	63·0
1969	0·3	29·1	5·9	64·7
South East Standard Region				
1951	3·3	30·7	6·9	59·1
1961	2·3	32·2	7·1	58·4
1966	1·6	32·5	6·9	59·0
1969	1·4	32·2	6·0	60·4
England and Wales				
1951	8·6	35·8	6·3	49·3
1961	6·4	36·8	6·8	50·0
1966	4·3	38·4	7·0	50·3
1969	3·6	38·7	6·4	51·3

* London conurbation.

Source: Greater London Council, *Greater London Development Plan: Public Inquiry Proof,* E11/1, London, October 1972, p. 23.

Second, there is the predominantly urban nature of the tertiary and quaternary activities in terms of their locational preferences relative to those of the primary and secondary activities. While there has been some degree of decentralisation of manufacturing, wholesale, and purely local retail and commercial activities to the periphery of large urban agglomerations and from the latter to smaller towns or even isolated villages, higher grade tertiary and the quaternary activities still tend markedly to centralise in the largest urban centres and in selected medium-sized cities or urban areas with relatively high levels of accessibility and amenity-based environmental attributes. This urban orientation is revealed in Table 3.7 by the declining shares and growth in shares of the service or tertiary sector as one proceeds outward from the urbanised core of Greater London, through the relatively highly urbanised area of the South-East, and finally to the average figures for the whole of England and Wales. By contrast, the shares of manufacturing activity are moving in the opposite direction with smaller and declining shares in Greater London, slightly higher but static shares in the South-East, and higher and slightly rising shares for England and Wales as a whole.

The crux of these policy issues, or perhaps dilemmas, is how one goes about placing the greatest number of people possible in living and working environments that provide accessibility to reasonably defined job advancement, educational, socio-cultural, and physical amenity attributes. These are much more demanding policy requirements than earlier regional economic efforts have set themselves. The question is no longer simply one of providing an unemployed or underemployed semi-skilled manufacturing worker with a manufacturing job in a manufacturing town that will not change in character or potential in the foreseeable future. The problems associated with redistributing the promising tertiary–quaternary office jobs and the attendant public infrastructure and services from congested agglomerations to locales with currently low but potentially high future opportunity are at the heart of the current reorientation of policy implementation strategies from regional economic amelioration to urban growth guidance that serves economic, social, and physical environmental ends. By focusing on the way in which these problems are being approached, we are able to evaluate the leading edge of innovation in the application of urban growth policy instruments in our study countries.

4 Trends and Hypotheses in Urban Growth and Distribution

What do the temporally and spatially dynamic growth forces and their resulting distribution of people and activities look like? This is a reasonable question to pose at the point when one wishes to know what any set of public policy instruments must work with or against in order to move towards desired aims. It also turns out to be an exceedingly complex and confounding question to answer, especially when operationally useful detail is required for policy application guidance. Even from the initial overview of urban growth trends we are confronted with the descriptive label of 'concentrated decentralisation', which attempts to capture their dichotomous nature in a single phrase.

From the first standpoint, concentrated decentralisation can be viewed as describing the continued expansion at lower densities of our existing large urban agglomerations or areas, i.e. the concentric expansion of dominant monocentric cities, such as Paris, London or New York, that have engulfed smaller cities and towns in their surrounding hinterlands, or the coalescence of adjacent cities, such as the Randstad or Rhine–Ruhr, the peripheral expansion of which has produced interlocking polycentric agglomerations. As long as growth is taking place in the context of a unified commuting shed linking jobs and residences and under a sphere of externality influence that ties people and activities to the dominant centre or centres for a variety of purposes, we are speaking of the growth or expansion of a single urban area according to our previous definition. As noted earlier by the commuting graphs in Figure 3.6, these central/peripheral organisational tendencies exert themselves even in the built-up maze of megalopolis. The main difference here is that the individual decision-making unit – household, firm, or public body – can make the choice, in areas of commuting-shed overlap, whether to orient toward one dominant centre or another or to divide its loyalty among centres over a period of time.

From the second standpoint, we can extend the concept of concentrated decentralisation to include explanation of the way in which people and activities disperse from the larger urban areas (and from rural or other 'non-urban' regions) to selected kinds of moderately large, medium, or smaller urban areas. We shall refer to this kind of growth distribution as 'dispersal', which, in fact, constitutes *migration* from one area to reconcentration in another. This description implies that growth is occurring in a great many different kinds of places in different locations. But this growth is selective according to definite patterns and not occurring randomly in all kinds of places.

Major features of the growth trends

The paucity of empirical research offers little to date in the way of verification of any central set of urban growth hypotheses, let alone a theory of urban growth. What is known about the basic structure and dynamics of these urban growth and distribution trends is best embodied in Berry's work and summarised in his own words that:

> There are two major elements in the city-centred organisation of economic activities in space that are important: (a) *a system of cities*, arranged in a hierarchy according to the functions performed by each; (b) corresponding *areas of urban influence* surrounding each of the cities in the system.
>
> We know the following about this system of spatial organisation:
>
> (a) The size and functions of a central city, the size of its urban field, and the spatial extent of developmental 'spread effects' radiating outward from it are proportional.
> (b) Impulses of economic change are transmitted in order from higher to lower centres in the urban hierarchy, in a 'size-rachet' sequence, so that continued innovation in large cities remains critical for extension of growth over the complete economic system.
> (c) The spatial incidence of economic growth is a function of distance from the central city. Troughs of economic backwardness lie in the most inaccessible areas along the peripheries between the least accessible lower-level centres in the hierarchy.
> (d) The growth potential of an area situated along an axis between two cities is a function of the intensity of interaction between them.[1]

The form, structure, and behaviour of 'systems of cities' and 'areas of urban influence' as described and observed by Berry lend credence to our contention that something called 'urban' growth policy can and should exist as an organiser of instrument application. First, however, we need to evaluate some key elements of urban growth and change to identify the points of leverage (or frustration) for policy intervention in what Berry calls the 'city-centred' territorial organisation of activities.

In countries where urbanisation of rural and small town populations has been largely completed, we find that the largest urban agglomerations have already begun to slow in rate of growth or even to decline in absolute terms. The marginal rates of population growth for such areas in England dropped significantly between the 1950s and the first half of the 1960s, as seen in Table 4.1. The rates of positive growth were relatively low in the 1950s and became predominantly negative in the early 1960s.

Table 4.1

Change in English conurbation populations, 1951 to 1966

Conurbation	Population 1951	Population 1961	Percentage change 1951–61	Population 1966	Percentage change 1961–66
Greater London	8,348,023	7,997,234	−4·2	7,671,220	−4·1
South East Lancs	2,422,650	2,427,919	+0·2	2,404,100	−1·0
West Midlands	2,237,095	2,378,005	+6·3	2,374,070	−0·2
West Yorkshire	1,692,687	1,703,678	+0·6	1,708,260	+0·3
Merseyside	1,382,443	1,384,198	+0·1	1,337,530	−3·4
Tyneside	835,533	855,295	+2·4	832,230	−2·7

Note: Unadjusted for London to ensure basis of comparison with other areas.

Source: Greater London Council – E11/1, op. cit., p. 19.

The implication appears to be that we are moving from further internal decentralisation and lowering of central densities in these largest urban agglomerations to dispersal of population from them to other areas. For the London area during the past decade it has, in fact, remained a combination of decentralisation from Central London to the periphery of what we would define as the London urban area, and dispersal to independent centres, as shown by the population changes in Table 4.2 for the 1960s. Greater London is the area within the Green Belt, the hiatus of strict development control surrounding London, while the Outer Metropolitan Area (OMA) is the next concentric ring of urban growth outside the belt. From our definitional viewpoint, significant proportions of OMA growth are still linked to Greater London through commuting or various functional interdependencies and therefore constitute continued expansion of the larger agglomeration.

41

Table 4.2

Mid-year estimates of resident population (millions)

	1961	1966	1969	1971	1972
Greater London	7·977	7·832	7·703	7·418	7·354
Outer Metropolitan Area	4·504	4·989	5·225	5·344	5·408
Outer South East	3·865	4·185	4·366	4·497	4·570
South East region	16·346	17·006	17·295	17·259	17·332

Source: Department of the Environment, *Strategic Planning in the South-east,* First Report of the Monitoring Group, DOE, London, March 1973, p. 26.

The remainder of growth at the outer fringes of the OMA and in the Outer South East (OSE) is taking place in relatively independent centres of growth and could be termed dispersal from the London area. The distinction between centres that are potentially independent or not in terms of frequent daily interaction with Greater London has much relevance for the type, form, and level of instrument application under alternative strategies of policy implementation. These policy issues are scrutinised, in terms of desirable and feasible implementation strategies for guiding instrument application, in the next section.

The expectations of the strategic planners in Britain are for a continuation of the trend of decentralisation in the London urban area, as evidenced by the projections for Greater London and the OMA in Figures 4.1 and 4.2. Likewise, a continued dispersal of population to the OSE is projected in Figure 4.3. The differences between the projection curves in each case are rooted mainly in varying assumptions about net in- and out-migration rates. These latter could be affected, of course, by future changes in policy as well as otherwise determined alterations in migration behaviour.

In countries with somewhat later industrialisation and urbanisation, the largest agglomerations are still capturing the highest proportion of national population growth and redistribution as exemplified by the Swedish experience graphed in Figure 4.4. Over the past century, Stockholm has risen to pre-eminence as it has come to contain nearly 20 per cent of national population as against about 7 per cent in 1870. Figure 4.5 displays the recent pattern of net migration that has been feeding the process of urban growth in the major centres of Sweden. Stockholm's predomi-

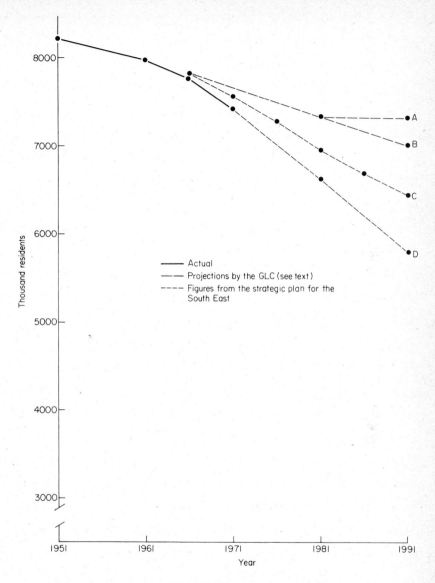

Fig. 4.1   Comparison of projections for Greater London.

Source: Eric J. Thompson, 'Some implications of recent population trends for South East England' *GLC Intelligence Bulletin* no. 22, March 1973, p. 40.

43

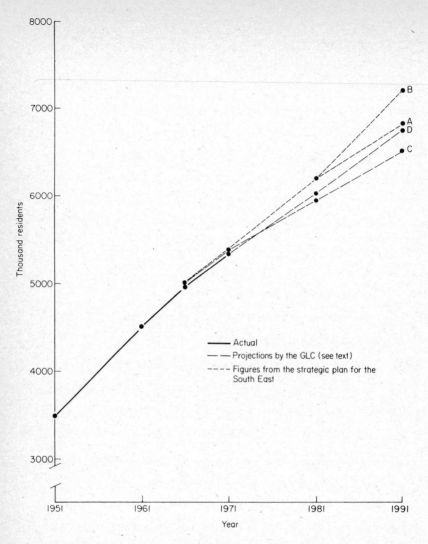

Fig. 4.2　Comparisons of projections for the Outer Metropolitan Area.

Source: Thompson, op. cit., p. 40.

nance is evident, but it is heavily dependent on flows from rural areas and relatively smaller urban places. Göteborg and Malmö contribute virtually nothing to Stockholm's growth according to these charts but, rather, in their own turn draw heavily from their surrounding regions and, in the case of Malmö, from Stockholm itself.

In a larger, and in many ways more diverse, country such as France, the dominance of the now massive Paris agglomeration is striking. It is diffi-

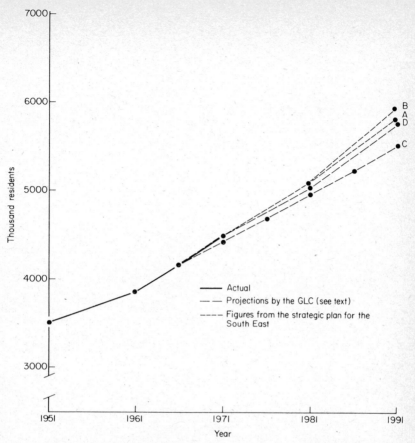

Fig. 4.3   Comparison of projections for the Outer South East.

Source: Thompson, op. cit., p. 41.

cult, however, to treat the growth in relative importance of Paris as the
result of a 'natural' trend that is devoid of governmental influence. If we
trace the dramatic rise in influence of Paris, as charted in Table 4.3, we
can readily perceive the historical association between the Napoleonic
centralisation of administration with its attendant power and authority
and the rapidly rising share of national population accumulating in Paris
during the nineteenth and early twentieth centuries. This oft-cited concur-
rence of historical events is usually offered simply as a unique example of
the peculiarities of French cultural orientation toward having the glory of
France reflected in the magnificence of Paris. But it provides an even more
pertinent example of the power of a consistently followed policy of locational preference to influence urban growth and distribution in a profound

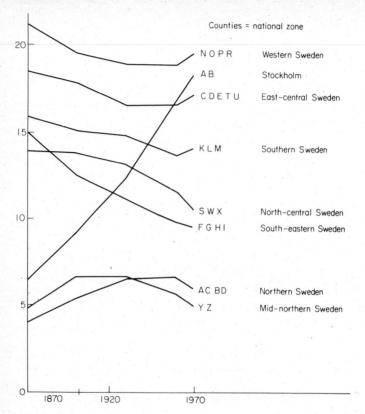

Percentage of population

Counties = national zone

N O P R	Western Sweden
A B	Stockholm
C D E T U	East-central Sweden
K L M	Southern Sweden
S W X	North-central Sweden
F G H I	South-eastern Sweden
AC BD	Northern Sweden
Y Z	Mid-northern Sweden

Fig. 4.4   Population distribution by national zones, 1870–1970.

Source: Swedish Ministry of Labour, op. cit., p. 3.

manner. Official French policy is now to soften — if reverse is too strong a word — this trend of a century and a half, and the lessons from the past are twofold: (1) many diverse activities (and public policy instruments) must be *co-ordinated* in some fashion to generate sufficient influence for balanced growth; and (2) the pursuit of this broadly based policy must be followed *consistently* over a lengthy period of time to establish and reinforce the desired locational tendencies.

While the total Paris agglomeration continues to grow in size, it displays a maturity in pattern of growth similar to that of London. Decentralisation is in full swing with the city of Paris declining in absolute terms and the peripheral portions of the urban area growing at successively greater rates as one proceeds outward from the centre. These changes are portrayed in Table 4.4.

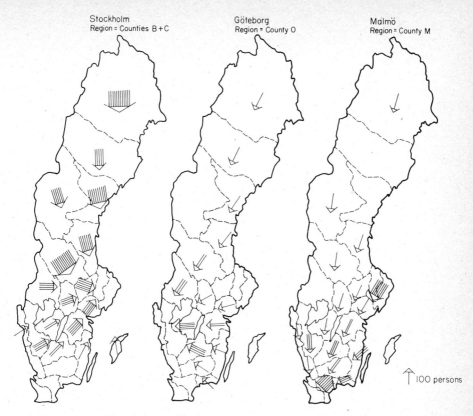

Fig. 4.5   Net migration flows to the three metropolitan regions of Sweden, 1966.

Source: Odmann and Dahlberg, op. cit., p. 45.

If we step beyond the Paris agglomeration itself to the potentially independent centres of growth surrounding it in the Paris Basin, we find a pattern of growth much in accordance with Berry's hypotheses set forth earlier. As one moves downward from the outlying agglomerations with higher growth rates to those with lower ones (see Table 4.5), the tendency is to find oneself moving consistently farther away from Paris and its externality influence, with only two or three major exceptions. For each average increment of distance gained from Paris, the average growth rate for the outlying areas is halved. Dispersal, then, is redounding to the benefit of many of these cities in the 'crown' adorning Paris.

Moving to the national level in France brings us to a view of the competitive force of the provincial metropolises and urban areas *vis-à-vis* Paris. Eight of the larger centres, or a grouping of adjacent centres in some cases,

Table 4.3

Evolution of the population of Paris and France, 1801–1965 (in millions)

		1801	1901	1921	1931	1946	1954	1962	1965
1	Paris	1·403	4·816	5·769	6·797	6·691	7·424	8·597	9·117
2	France	27·350	40·862	39·210	41·834	40·502	42·502	46·520	48·699
1 as a per cent of 2		5·1	11·8	14·7	16·2	16·5	17·5	18·5	18·7

Source: Niles M. Hansen, *French Regional Planning,* Indiana University Press, Bloomington 1968, p. 29.

Table 4.4

The population of the Paris agglomeration

	Population change 1962–68		Change due to migration
	1968	%	%
Paris city	2,581,796	−7·0	−10·2
Inner suburban ring			
North	557,913	9·8	3·3
East	756,226	6·6	1·7
South	826,748	8·5	4·1
West	870,232	5·0	− 1·5
Outer suburban ring			
North	530,777	33·6	26·1
East	610,900	27·2	20·4
South	864,127	37·7	30·2
West	583,522	21·7	15·3
Total agglomeration	8,182,241	7·9	2·9

Source: Ian B. Thompson, *The Paris Basin,* Oxford University Press, London 1973, p. 13.

Table 4.5

Population change in the major agglomerations of the Paris Basin by growth rates and distance from Paris

Agglomeration	Rate of change %	Migration rate %	Distance from Paris in kilometres
Mantes	38·5	28·5	60
Creil	36·7	29·2	50
Melun	29·3	19·8	45
Caen	25·8	16·6	227
Tours	22·5	16·8	235
Châlons–s–Marne	22·1	13·1	160
Chartres	21·4	14·8	94
Average for high group	*28·0*	*19·8*	*110*
Orléans	18·7	11·8	115
Reims	16·8	10·3	154
Bourges	16·7	11·6	224
Le Mans	14·0	6·2	215
Troyes	13·4	7·9	160
Rouen	12·7	5·3	140
Amiens	12·7	5·7	131
Nevers	10·5	6·4	236
Charleville–Mézières	10·2	2·6	237
Average for middle group	*14·1*	*7·5*	*179*
Cherbourg	9·6	1·6	346
Le Havre	9·5	3·4	226
St. Quentin	6·9	1·0	140
Châteauroux	5·0	−1·0	251
Average for low group	*7·8*	*1·3*	*241*

Source: Thompson, op. cit., p. 19.

have been designated as *métropoles d'équilibre* with the express roles of acting as counterpoints to the growth of Paris. In spite of continued Parisian growth, the relative performance of the *métropoles* during the 1960s was favourable as pointed out in Table 4.6. All but one of the *métropoles* experienced growth rates ranging from several percentage points higher than Paris up to two and nearly three times as great.

In this discussion of trends we have seen patterns of growth favouring moderately large independent metropolitan areas such as the *métropoles d'équilibre*, smaller or medium-sized urban areas in relatively favourable

Table 4.6

Population change in the major agglomerations of France, 1962–68

Paris and the *métropoles d'équilibre*	Population		Growth index, 1968/1962.
	1962	1968	1962 = 100
Paris	*7,323,000*	*7,822,000*	*107*
Bordeaux	498,429	555,152	111
Lille–Roubaix–Tourcoing	821,228	881,439	107
Lyon–St. Etienne–Grenoble	1,520,859	1,738,660	114
Marseille–Aix–Fos	909,911	1,056,847	116
Nancy–Metz–Thionville	508,783	560,657	110
Nantes–Saint Nazaire	453,632	504,628	111
Strasbourg	302,772	334,668	111
Toulouse	365,482	439,764	120

Source: INSEE and DATAR, *Statistiques et indicateurs des régions françaises,* Projet de loi de finances pour 1971, Paris, p. 36; and the Institut d'amenagement et d'urbanisme de la région parisienne, *Hypothèse population-actifs-emplois 1975, et 1985–90,* Paris, March 1972.

positions adjacent to the largest agglomerations, such as the cities of the South East of Britain and the Paris Basin and the outermost portions of the largest agglomerations, even though the latter tend to be declining in their total rates of growth. Can we discern any significant association between size of urban area and rate of growth? Berry has produced an interesting graph relating size and growth for DUS (i.e. 'daily urban systems', which approximate our definition of urban area) in the United States during the last decade. The results are depicted in Figure 4.6 from which we can see and conclude that:

> The median population growth rate of successive size classes of DUS's increased progressively with size to a population of 1,000,000, and stabilized thereafter at about the national growth rate. This is consistent with ideas of the relationship of size to self-generative growth.
> ... realisation of scale and agglomeration economies no longer produces a greater-than-average growth rate of the largest DUS's. Instead, at larger sizes there is convergence on the growth rate of the nation ...

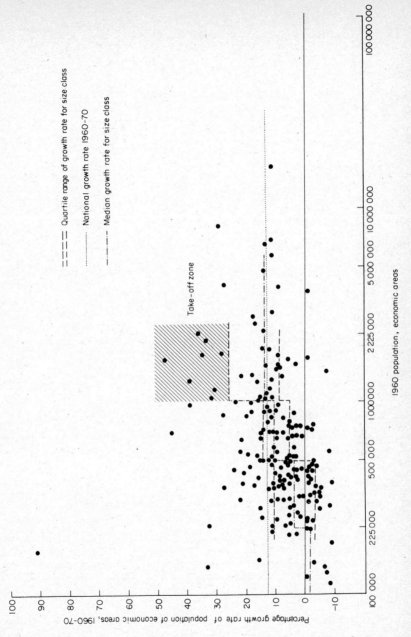

Fig. 4.6   Relationship of the population growth rate of USA daily urban systems, 1960–70, to their size in 1960.

Source: B. J. L. Berry, 'Contemporary urbanization processes', mimeo, National Academy of Sciences, Washington DC, September 1971, p. 26.

The inter-quartile range was stable for size classes of less than 1,000,000, and above that point also for the lower quartile. However, the upper quartile was markedly greater than elsewhere in the size class 1,000,000–2,225,000 indicating an accelerated 'take-off' of many economic areas of this size range in particular ...

The median growth rate was negative in the smallest size class, as was the lower quartile in the size range 225,000–500,000, indicating that declining DUS's are disproportionately the smaller ones ... focussing on lower-status wholesale-retail centres ...

On the other hand, from a size of 1,000,000 downwards, there is a progressive decline in the growth rate with decreasing size and, presumably, lessening urban economies. Deviations from this declining growth rate are associated with increasing productivity and resource depletion in the primary industries on the one hand, and with the rise of the service sector and the haphazard pattern of fallout governmental expenditures on the other hand.[2]

The absolute levels of population or activities that constitute 'large' agglomerations, 'moderate/medium-sized' cities, or 'small' urban areas and towns are in themselves relative concepts. They must be determined in the context of each national system of cities, viz. the different orders of magnitude in sizes of London and Paris versus Stockholm or, for 'moderate' sized areas, the differences between Birmingham, Manchester and Lyon versus Malmö and Göteborg. Even though absolute sizes need to be 'normalised' for comparisons between different national contexts, Berry's conclusions about urban areas in various relative positions in the national hierarchies may have greater general validity.

The implications are that we need not expect continued high levels of growth and concentration in the very largest urban agglomerations. At the other extreme, we ought not to anticipate much in the way of rapid growth, or perhaps any growth at all, from urban areas in the lowest one or two size classes; especially 'balanced' growth that replicates the development pattern of our present larger metropolitan areas that have wide ranges of activities and opportunities present in them. In between 'large' and 'small', presumably we find a variety of candidates for accelerated growth where application of policy could obtain sizeable amounts of leverage. In the United States, this appears to mean urban areas of 'moderately large' size which translates into a population range of one to two and one-quarter million. The *métropoles d'équilibre* would constitute roughly this same relative size class in France, which translates into an urban area population size range of about one-half to one and one-half million.

For purposes of determining places and types of specific policy intervention, it is the nature and incidence of some of the deviations from this consistent pattern and the hypotheses explaining the resulting extreme growth values that are most interesting. Even though median values of growth rates are below the national average for size classes from 225,000 one million in Figure 4.6, we can see many observations positioned well above the average. Some of these may have resulted from unique historical advantages which have no particular lesson or relevance for public policy since they arise from factors that could not be controlled or replicated through instruments available to the latter, e.g. unique natural amenity. Given the fact of their existence, however, policy could capitalise on or protect those advantages, e.g. develop recreational facilities versus creation of nature conservancies. More consistent operational value, then, is derived from specifying the key growth factors in the urbanisation process that can be influenced through discretionary use of available policy instruments, e.g. service sector (tertiary—quaternary) activities and various forms of governmental expenditure. Berry's analysis has, on the face of it, shown these latter two factors to have a relevance which our subsequent treatment of policy strategies and instruments and their innovative use reveals is becoming increasingly recognised in those countries that are attempting actively to influence urban growth and distribution in beneficial ways.

Geographic shifts by offices and quaternary functions: changing opportunity structures

The movement of tertiary and quaternary jobs and activities, reflected largely but not entirely by the distribution of office locations, defines even more clearly the interwoven trends of urban dispersal and reconcentration. It is estimated that somewhere between 124,000 and 168,000 office jobs moved from the central or core area of Greater London to other locations between 1963 and 1969.[3] The pattern of these moves is suggested by the data on distance moved from Central London given in Table 4.7, based on sample information. The heavy preponderance of firms moving from the centre and remaining within the Greater London Council area, i.e. inside the Green Belt, is striking indeed — over one-half of all jobs. If one includes all office jobs moved that remained within a 40-mile radius of the centre, perhaps approximating the outer commuting range, about three-quarters of all the moves are accounted for.

It is clear that, in moving from the highly congested core of the London agglomeration, office firms are minimising their externality loss by yield-

Table 4.7

Distances moved by decentralisers from Central London, 1963–69

	Complete moves		Partial moves 50+		Partial moves under 50		Government moves	Total of jobs			
	Upper	Lower	Upper	Lower	Upper	Lower		Upper		Lower	
								(No.)	(%)	(No.)	(%)
GLC Area	53,639	33,172	26,342	20,905	7,545	5,937	3,065	90,591	55.8	63,079	52.8
GLC – 19 miles	5,722	3,538	1,549	1,230	2,434	1,915	30	9,735	6.0	6,713	5.6
20–39 miles	5,722	3,538	10,330	8,198	7,545	5,937	2,480	26,077	16.0	20,153	16.9
40–59 miles	2,860	1,770	1,549	1,230	2,920	2,298	1,180	8,509	5.2	6,478	5.4
60–79 miles	1,430	884	3,099	2,459	1,704	1,341	1,194	7,427	4.6	5,878	4.9
80+	2,146	1,327	8,781	6,968	2,191	1,724	7,110	20,228	12.4	17,129	14.4
Totals	71,519	44,229	51,650	40,990	24,339	19,152	15,059	162,567	100.0	119,430	100.0

Notes: The totals exclude the 5,000 jobs attributed to the nationalised industries.

It is assumed that each firm took the same number of jobs as other firms in its category.

The totals are calculated by analysing the distance moved by the firms in the samples.

The upper and lower figures given are the respective limits of the confidence intervals at the 99 per cent level of certainty based on samples of London firms and central government departments.

Source: R. K. Hall, 'The movement of offices from Central London' *Regional Studies* vol. 6, no. 4, December 1972, p. 390.

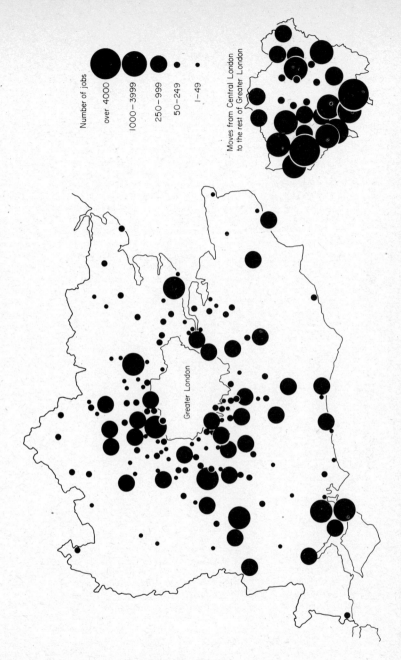

Fig. 4.7   Destination of office jobs moved from Greater London through the Location of Offices Bureau 1963–71.

Source: DOE, *Strategic Planning ...,* First Report ..., op. cit., p. 54a.

ing to centripetal pressures causing them either to adhere as closely as possible to the old dominant centre or to regroup in outlying centres of the South East with some links to London. The number of moves beyond the South East region itself constitutes a very small proportion of the total — about 15 per cent — and likely these were destined for selected medium to larger-sized cities elsewhere in Britain. The tightly grouped and individually concentrated pattern of office relocation is graphically displayed in Figure 4.7 for the South East region around Greater London and, by the small inset, for the GLC area itself. Greater London, in the setting of the South East, remains the dominant office centre, but with a more dispersed form of location within its boundaries. The Greater London Development Plan has taken this trend into account through its proposed support for 28 office/commercial centres scattered around the GLC.

The changes in occupational structure with office moves suggest selective socio-economic redistributions between areas. The question of who goes along when the firm and its jobs are moved is partially answered by the proportions of different classes of workers moving with their jobs in the South East during 1945–68 (see Table 4.8). The 'higher-level' or

Table 4.8

Mobile industry within South East England: transfer of employees by distance of move and type of employment, 1945–68

Distance moved in miles	Percentage of 'high-level' staff* to transfer with firm	Percentage of 'low-level' staff† to transfer with firm	Percentage of all staff to transfer with firm
5–10	88	61	75
11–20	85	55	68
21–40	69	29	41
41–60	55	18	30
61+	64	8	14
Total	70	33	43

* 'High-level' staff includes managers, supervisors, scientists, technologists and skilled production workers.
† 'Low-level' staff includes clerical, office, semi-skilled and unskilled production workers.

Source: EFTA, 'New patterns ...', op. cit., no page number.

quarternary type workers have a much greater tendency to move with firm and job, whether they stay in the same urban area or not. The 'lower-level' workers have a lower and more rapidly declining rate of adherence to firm and job with distance of move by the latter. This difference probably is largely explained by the difference in the two job markets — the quaternary worker being in a national job market for his skills, coupled with more career association to a firm, as against the routine tertiary or secondary-sector worker, who is in a local (particular urban area) job market for his skill, with association to an industry or industries potentially employing him and little or no career attachments to a given firm. The dependence of the latter on access to a large and varied labour market is obvious. But the changes in distribution of jobs in London, depicted in Table 4.9, seem to be working against the 'lower-level' workers who might be remaining in London after jobs have shifted out.

Table 4.9

Changes in managerial and clerical employment,
Greater London, 1961–66

Area	Administrative and professional office workers		Clerical office workers		All office workers		All occupations	
	1,000	%	1,000	%	1,000	%	1,000	%
Central London	+19	9	−16	−3	+ 3	−	− 65	−5
Rest of Greater London	+60	28	+65	15	+125	19	+131	4
Total for Greater London	+79	18	+49	5	+128	9	+ 66	2

Source: EFTA, op. cit., no page number.

Since quaternary-type office jobs increased by 18 per cent between 1961 and 1966 in Greater London, while tertiary types rose by only 5 per cent, we have an indication that the more routine kinds of tasks are being sloughed off to outlying centres with selective reinforcement of the more discretionary types of work in the dominant centre of the conurbation.

Defining the nature and strength of the functional processes producing the coalescence of tertiary-sector and quaternary functions across all sectors in quantifiable terms is a challenging task. Input—output matrices

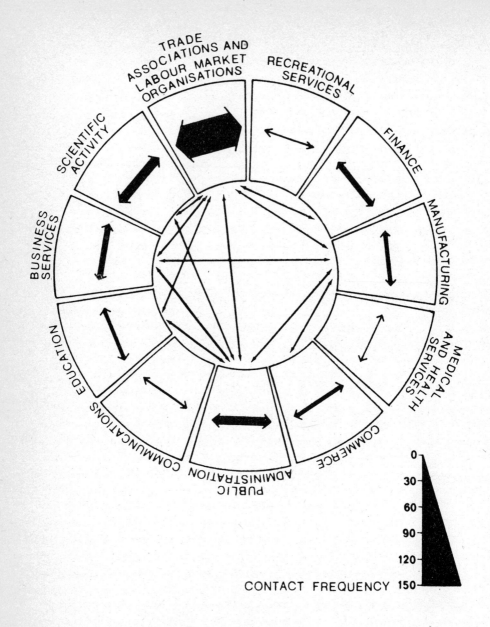

Fig. 4.8 The contact system – a summary.

Note: Personal contacts within and between industrial, trade and service sectors.

Source: Gunnar Törnquist, *Contact Systems and Regional Development,* C.W.K. Gleerup, Lund 1970, p. 83.

Table 4.10

The contact-intensity of industrial, trade and service sectors and the regional concentration of employment

Sectors ranked by contact-intensity		Percentage of total labour force engaged in Stockholm A-region in 1965
Trade associations and labour market organisations, etc.	(1)	58
Non-profit organisations	(2)	38
Research activities	(3)	70
Public administration	(4)	30
Business services	(5)	45
Libraries and museums	(6)	40
Financing	(7)	43
Education	(8)	21
Religious activities	(9)	14
Transport and communications	(10)	23
Recreational activities	(11)	25
Health and medical services	(12)	19
Commerce	(13)	22
Manufacturing	(14)	15
Social welfare	(15)	27
Agriculture	(16)	2

Source: Törnquist, op. cit., p. 94.

have been constructed, at great cost in effort and time, to measure the purchase/sale interdependencies of secondary (manufacturing) enterprises in the past. But in the service and transactional spheres the most valuable inputs and outputs are information, knowledge, judgement, and decision. The most effective measurement reduction and modelling of these interactions to date have been produced by the efforts of people like Törnquist[4] and Goddard.[5] The unit of measure is the number of contacts made between people in organisations in the different activity sectors. Figure 4.8 offers a simple graphical model showing the frequency of contact within and between major sectors. The convergence of arrows in the centre of the wheel from several other sectors on the public administrative sector suggests some degree of leverage or multiplicative effect attendant on the relocation of government offices, especially those with higher-level decision-making functions.

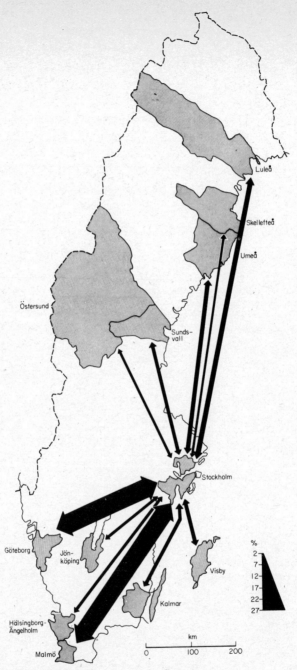

Fig. 4.9   The spatial contact pattern in Sweden.

Note: Percentage distribution of personal contacts between places of work in various A-regions with airports. (Combinations resulting in at least 2 per cent of the total.) (Sahlberg 1969.)   *Source:* Törnquist, op. cit., p. 79.

The proclivity of the higher-grade tertiary and quaternary functions to congregate in the largest urban areas because of strong mutual interdependencies is apparent in Table 4.10. The economic sectors are ranked by frequency or intensity of contact with other organisations in their own and other sectors. The requirements for spatial clustering in a high-externality environment are reflected in the higher proportions of national labour force found in Stockholm for each of the contact-intensive sectors, with labour force proportions declining in close accordance with reduction in contact-intensity ranking. These contact requirements work to produce the concentrated development pattern for Sweden displayed in Figure 4.9. The focus of all contacts on Stockholm and the distinct second-order importance of only two other metropolitan scale areas – Göteborg and Malmö – emphasises the selectivity of location and relative scarcity of adequate externality environments for the expanding tertiary and quaternary activities.

The implications for occupational structure and expanding socio-economic opportunity, as measured by income levels, in the urban areas of Sweden are suggested by the observed positive relationships between an-

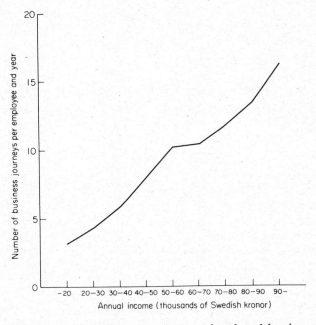

Fig. 4.10   The relationship between income level and business journeys in Sweden.

Source: Törnquist, op. cit., p. 68.

nual income and, respectively, number of business trips made and proportion of time spent in contact endeavours by employees (see Figs 4.10 and 4.11). The income-distributional effects of an urban area's ability to capture and generate contact-intensive quarternary jobs, as we can see in Table 4.11 are highly significant. Stockholm, Malmö and Göteborg, the three major centres of contact intensive employment, have lower than average shares of workers earning under 25,000 kronor per year, but progressively higher shares of those earning between 30,000 and over 50,000 kronor per year.

The still rapidly expanding New York agglomeration — considerably larger than the SMSA definition — has lost much resident population from its core and has seen further multinodal growth in its peripheral reaches.

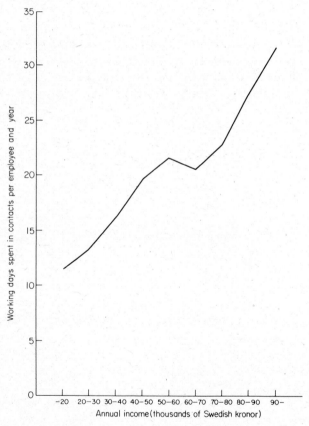

Fig. 4.11 The relationship between income level and time spent on contact activity in Sweden.

Source: Törnquist, op. cit., p. 68.

Concurrent with these changes, however, has been a continued mainte-nance of the number of jobs relative to people in Manhattan and the adjacent central area such that the old centre has not yielded the degree of its dominance in the overall urban region, as depicted by the jobs/people ratios computed in Table 4.12. The strength of these centralising tenden-cies in the tertiary and quaternary sectors is still tying millions of com-muters to Manhattan.

The pattern of activities locating or remaining in Manhattan is, again, a selective one. This is perhaps even more forcefully revealed by a recent study of manufacturing location behaviour in New York[6] than it would be by a study of office locations such as we recounted for London. In Table 4.13 we see the recent marginal changes in employment shares for those manufacturing industries that are increasing their concentration in Manhattan even while, overall, manufacturing is declining in its propor-tionate representation. These centralising secondary-sector activities all have specialised requirements for production of goods that are standard-ised in certain ways but highly unique and variable in other ways. There is a good deal of skilled judgement and consultation on specialised or styl-ised design — apparel and textiles and printing, for example — that causes these kinds of manufacturing tasks to gain comparative advantage from the rich web of interdependencies existing in such a place as Manhattan.

This argument is further supported by the relatively higher worker productivity in New York than in the United States in general for those activities gaining from such externality influence. This is shown by the comparisons of value added per employee in Table 4.14. With the excep-tion of machinery manufacture, those activities gaining in share of em-ployment in Manhattan also have higher than national average productivi-ty in their New York locations, and for printing and publishing there is a sizeable advantage. Categorisation and expectations of locational behav-iour of activities should be approached carefully, for, as Gottman has cautioned, 'The quaternary sector permeates not only the services but also some of the secondary sector. Publishing, for instance, is considered a manufacturing industry and therefore belongs in the secondary sector of economic activity. A large part however, perhaps the majority of employ-ment in publishing firms consists of managerial and editorial staff belong-ing rather in the quaternary sector'.[7]

If we elevate our view to the national level again and evaluate the competitive positions of urban areas by size, we find that the pattern of productivity advantage for larger urban areas is the same in general for all industries as it was in New York for our specialised cases. In Table 4.15, we see that Stockholm maintains a distinct productivity edge overall even

63

Table 4.11

Sweden: income distribution, 1967 (Swedish kronor)

Class of urban area	−5,000		5,001−10,000		10,001−15,000		15,001−20,000	
	No. (000)	%	No. (000)	%	No. (000)	%	No. (000)	%
National*	23	1·6	74	5·2	70	4·9	86	6·0
Sub-national†	21	1·9	80	7·1	68	6·0	112	9·9
Regional	64	2·5	211	8·2	201	7·8	342	13·3
Local	85	3·5	216	8·9	260	10·7	358	14·7
Whole country	208	2·6	657	8·2	673	8·4	994	12·4

* Stockholm.
† Malmö and Göteborg.

Source: EFTA, op. cit., no page number.

when we control successively for the variations in capital intensity, size of firm, and size of urban areas.

Finally, since we have suggested the linkage between occupational structure, together with the presence or absence of job advancement opportunity, and the socio-economic well-being of resident populations, we need to assess the degree of real income (money income adjusted for inflation and inter-area living cost differentials) gain accruing to people living in urban areas of different size and location. Recent analysis of urban area income distributions in the United States provides some insight. Looking first at undeflated per capita incomes for urban areas over about the past 40 years (see Table 4.16), we can discern a trend toward convergence as the index values of the largest areas decline and those of some smaller areas rise. But there are locational influences as well, since smaller SMSAs in the North remained relatively static in their index values while those in the South gained noticeably. However, at the end of the period the larger SMSAs still had significant income advantages, and progressively so with increase in size.

Turning to a comparison of deflated money income levels, from the index values in Table 4.17, arranged by size class of urban area and region, we still see a fairly steady rise in level of income as we move from urban areas under 10,000 population to agglomerations above one million. The only exception to this pattern is in the urban areas under one million population of the North-east region. The largest increment of deflated

20,001–30,000		25,001–30,000		30,001–40,000		40,001–50,000		50,001+	
No. (000)	%	No. (000)	%	No. (000)	%	No. (000)	%	No. (000)	%
138	9·7	190	13·3	355	24·9	238	16·7	252	17·7
150	13·3	142	12·6	281	24·9	159	14·1	114	10·1
427	16·6	394	15·3	494	19·2	260	10·1	180	7·0
396	16·3	345	14·2	433	17·8	209	8·6	134	5·5
1,202	15·0	1,114	13·9	1,611	20·1	882	11·0	673	8·4

income for all regions occurs between urban areas under a million and those over a million. The interpretation of these differences is a fairly open question at this juncture in our knowledge, and Hoch interprets it as a compensatory payment to the residents of huge agglomerations for the negative externalities (social or third-party costs) imposed on them and caused by congestion, environmental insults giving rise to ill health, poor social surroundings measured by crime rates, and so on.[8] We can make out as good a case for the argument that the positive association between size and deflated income is caused by higher productivity levels in larger urban areas.

What inferences can we draw now for policy guidance from the suggestive evidence and arguable, but often insufficiently tested, hypotheses that we have traced in our evaluation of growth trends? Perhaps at this awkward intermediate and incomplete stage of investigation of the nature and role of urban growth policy, we can only note, as Gottmann does, that:

> There is little doubt that the main international hubs of transactional activity, such as New York, Washington, London, Paris, Amsterdam, Tokyo, Moscow, are growing so big and so complex that they appear hardly manageable. Very little is known about the way they work. In the constantly self-refining and sub-dividing division of labour that now affects the masses of white-collar workers, some stages of work require presence in large hubs and others could be performed else-

65

Table 4.12

Population and jobs, by parts of the New York region, 1956 and 1965

Area	1956			1965		
	People (000)	Jobs (000)	Ratio	People (000)	Jobs (000)	Ratio
Manhattan, CBD	620	2,475	4·00			
Manhattan, all	1,811	2,718	1·50	1,565	2,406	1·54
Core	8,236	4,302	0·52	8,757	4,453	0·51
Inner Ring	4,573	1,572	0·34	4,655	1,568	0·34
Intermediate Ring	2,566	826	0·32	4,280	1,339	0·31
Outer Ring				1,290	407	0·32
Total	15,375	6,700	0·43	18,981	7,796	0·41

Note: These areas are not strictly comparable for the two sources and time periods; their definitions are as follows:

	1956	1965
Core	Manhattan, Hudson, Brooklyn, Queens, Bronx	Manhattan, Hudson, Brooklyn, Queens, Bronx, City of Newark
Inner Ring	Richmond, Essex, Bergen, Passaic, Westchester, Union, Nassau	Richmond, Essex West, Bergen, Passaic South, Westchester South, Union, Nassau
Intermediate Ring	Middlesex, Rockland, Morris, Monmouth, Somerset, Fairfield, Suffolk, Orange, Putnam, Dutchess	Fairfield South, Middlesex, Suffolk West, Mercer, New Haven, Rockland, Monmouth, Morris, Westchester North, Somerset, Passaic North
Outer Ring		Fairfield North, Suffolk East, Dutchess, Ocean, Warren, Putnam, Hunterdon, Litchfield, Orange, Ulster, Sussex, Sullivan

Source: Marion Clawson, *Suburban Land Conversion in the United States,* The Johns Hopkins Press, Baltimore 1971, p. 271.

Table 4.13

Major industries increasingly concentrated in Manhattan, 1967 and 1969
(Manhattan's share of SMSA employment in per cent)

Industry	1967	1969
All manufacturing	*42·1*	*41·4*
Textile mill products	41·9	43·3
Apparel	70·6	74·0
Printing	72·5	74·4
Machinery, non-electric	15·9	17·7
Electric machinery	15·1	17·3
Instruments	13·3	17·7

Source: Robert A. Leone, 'Location of manufacturing activity in the New York metropolitan area', National Bureau of Economic Research, Inc., New York, no date, p. 71.

Table 4.14

Value added per employee, United States and New York SMSA, by major industries in New York SMSA, 1963 and 1967, US dollars

Industry	New York		United States	
	1963	1967	1963	1967
Food and kindred products	14,074	16,780	13,300	15,932
Textile mill products	8,985	10,397	7,096	8,596
Apparel	8,115	8,713	6,146	7,112
Printing and publishing	15,978	19,030	11,461	13,303
Chemicals	24,281	26,970	23,860	27,740
Fabricated metals	9,805	11,505	10,898	13,048
Machinery, non-electrical	11,311	13,709	11,837	14,795
Electrical machinery	10,180	12,409	11,258	13,192
+39 misc. and ordinance	8,410	10,700	9,913	11,961
Total	9,953	12,034	11,321	13,374

Source: Leone, op. cit., p. 182.

Table 4.15

Industrial productivity by hierarchical level of urban units, standardised for capital intensity, size of firm and size of urban unit, Sweden 1968

	A	B	C	D
National*	109·6	108·7	108·3	104·9
Sub-national†	104·1	101·7	101·0	99·8
Regional	102·9	100·3	99·3	98·5
Local	97·0	98·3	97·8	98·3
All Sweden	100·0	100·0	100·0	100·0

Note: A: Value added per employee.
      B: Value added standardised by capital intensity.
      C: Value added standardised by capital intensity and size of firm.
      D: Value added standardised by capital intensity, size of firm and size of urban unit.

* Stockholm.
† Malmö and Göteborg.

Source: EFTA, 'New patterns ...', op. cit., no page number.

where. What can be decentralised and to where is a question which has been little studied in terms of general principles. The practice has chiefly been to forbid new building for certain uses in certain zones, and this restrictive zoning or prohibitive legislation was first applied to manufactures and warehouses, then to offices. While pressure was exerted to push some employment out, incentives were provided either by the central government or by local government, and sometimes by both, to bring the moving activities to areas or places of lagging growth, or even economic decline. It may be time to investigate the situation in cities of intermediate size (that is, with populations of between 100,000 and 1,500,000) and see how these communities work in terms of urban centrality. Such cities may be able to receive easily new industrial plants and warehouses, but it may be much more difficult for them to accommodate quaternary activities.[9]

We turn now to a concise scrutiny of the operational strategies for policy implementation that have arisen in response to some of the challenges to

Table 4.16

Index of per capita income, over time by SMSA population group and region

Population group, 1960	Mean index of per capita income, US Average = 100							
	1929	1940	1950	1959	1962	1965	1966	1967
New York SMSA	195	167	140	144	138	136	134	135
SMSAs over 2 million (9 cases)	150	149	126	128	122	121	121	120
Northern SMSAs								
1 million – 2 million (11 cases)	134	133	122	125	118	117	117	117
300,000 – 400,000 (9 cases)	107	113	110	108	99	99	98	99
100,000 – 200,000 (41 cases)	101	101	105	107	102	101	100	100
Below 100,000 (9 cases)	104	109	109	110	104	101	100	102
Southern SMSAs								
1 million – 2 million (3 cases)	108	113	117	115	107	105	104	105
300,000 – 400,000 (7 cases)	79	89	92	95	87	87	89	89
100,000 – 200,000 (21 cases)	71	74	84	85	79	80	81	82
Below 100,000 (13 cases)	70	75	84	83	79	82	82	83
Sum of all SMSA counties	132	129	117	113	112	111	111	111
Sum of all non-SMSA areas	57	59	73	74	76	77	77	77

Source: Irving Hoch, 'Income and city size' *Urban Studies* vol. 9, no. 3, October 1972, p. 314.

Table 4.17

Deflated* money income levels for standardised population, 1966

Locale, population in thousands	Assumed average	Deflated wage rate			
	Population size in thousands	North-east	North-central	South	West
Urban place					
< 10	5	0·984	0·921	0·869	0·957
10– < 100	50	0·979	0·975	0·928	0·990
SMSA					
< 250	125	0·973	1·064	0·986	1·033
250– < 500	375	0·953	1·045	1·028	1·003
500– <1,000	750	0·970	1·111	1·042	1·039
1,000+	2,000	1·056	1·119	1·122	1·106
1,000+ relative to (<10)		1·073	1·215	1·291	1·156

* Deflated by a cost-of-living index for inter-area differences.

Source: Hoch, p. 311.

the quality of urban living posed by the nature and direction of the trends described.

Notes

[1] Berry, *Transactions ...*, op. cit., p. 43.

[2] Berry, 'Contemporary urbanization processes', mimeo, National Academy of Sciences, Washington DC, September 1971, pp. 11 and 13.

[3] R. K. Hall, 'The movement of offices from Central London' *Regional Studies* vol. 6, no. 4, December 1972, p. 389.

[4] Gunnar Törnquist, *Contact Systems and Regional Development*, C. W. K. Gleerup, Lund 1970.

[5] John B. Goddard, 'Information flows and the development of the urban system: theoretical considerations and policy implications', Paper prepared for the Urban Economics Conference of the Centre for Environmental Studies, 10–13 July 1973, University of Keele, England.

[6] Robert A. Leone, 'Location of manufacturing activity in the New

York Metropolitan Area', National Bureau of Economic Research, Inc., New York, no date.

[7] Gottmann, op. cit., p. 325.

[8] Irving Hoch, 'Income and city size' *Urban Studies* vol. 9, no. 3, October 1972, pp. 299–328.

[9] Gottmann, op. cit., p. 328.

5 National Policy Responses and Feasible Implementation Strategies

How, in fact, have national governments responded with implementation approaches for policies that are caught in the crucible between the earlier-enunciated policy concerns and the urban growth trends just described? It would be spurious for us to set forth an arbitrarily defined set of 'consistent' urban growth objectives from which policies and strategies could flow neatly because, rather, we desire to keep the analysis and evaluation rooted in the actual states of policy development in the respective study countries. But there is definite benefit to be gained from briefly canvassing the most recent government statements of objectives in order to derive a reasonably unified concept of the actual aims and directions that policy applications are taking on.

The emerging urban growth policy focus as reflected in national goals

The increasing orientation towards *urban* growth policy is being derived from reorientation of earlier regional, physical environmental, and urban 'form and structuring' efforts. We find that in Sweden, for, example, what is still referred to under the generic title of 'regional policy' has come to be aimed at the following comprehensive, and, according to the realities of the earlier-recounted growth trends, urban growth objectives:

> ... the Swedish regional policy is to bring an efficient utilisation of available factors of production and an increase in economic growth into gear with an improved geographical balance in the development of economic activity. In that way regional policy aims at an increased economic, social and cultural equality between people in different regions. Another objective is to provide security for the individual during the process of structural change and economic expansion ...
>
> The general objectives were made more concrete in a proposal to the Parliament on regional policy in the autumn of 1972. According

to the ensuing decisions of the Parliament, the regional structure should be designed according to people's needs with respect to three essential welfare components: work, services, and good environment. The aim is to build up, in various economic-geographic regions, places that complement each other *in such a way* that these welfare components can be universally attained ...

The aim of the regional development planning was to create an effective infrastructure in terms of schools, hospitals, roads and other communications and public services. The state, the municipalities and the business community should co-operate in such a way as to make possible concentrated efforts in suitable places.[1]
[Author's italics.]

Reflecting this expansion of growth objectives is the work underway to redefine, for policy implementation purposes, the types of areas to serve as the foci for growth — moving away from large regions to recognition of four basic levels of urban area: (1) metropolitan areas; (2) primary centres; (3) regional centres; and (4) local centres.[2]

The Netherlands took an early lead in joining the control of Randstad growth with stimulation of sizeable alternative urban areas. As far back as the early 1950s it was recognised that more comprehensive objectives were necessary to produce desirable and meaningful results from implementation measures. In the attempt to stimulate growth in the north of the country as a counterpoint to the Randstad, the government position has become that:

... what is especially wrong there is the absence of a single, varied, large, urban agglomeration, which can serve as the economic motor for a vast area, and, among other things, on account of its varied labour market can exert a great force of attraction of new industry of a more than regional importance and of a modern character. In view of this the accent has been placed on the reinforcement of a single complex: Groningen–Delfzijl–Eemshaven ... it places the emphasis on the promotion of a differentiated industrial structure, interacting with the formation of a really urban environment.[3]

There seems to be an intention to capitalise on the externalities of city-centred growth rather than just the more narrowly defined job multipliers of inter-plant linkages in the manufacturing sector.

Perhaps few other countries have as rich a modern history of urban and regional policies, or of programmes to effect them, as does the United Kingdom. At the national level three major policies and programme efforts converge on the issues of urban growth:

> ... these are the Green Belt, New and Expanded Towns, and Regional Economic policies.
> ... Green Belt policy is intended mainly to effect the containment of large urban areas. New and Expanded Towns were originally intended to achieve the co-ordinated decentralisation of population and employment from overcrowded conurbations, but they have become increasingly important as outlets for the growth of population generally and are used as instruments of Regional Economic policy, which attempts to secure a better distribution of employment opportunities in the country; this also indirectly affects broad population distribution. ... In all the policies ... there has been a process of evolution from the early post-war period, when objectives were limited, to today's broader, more flexible policies, which are seen as being interrelated and complementing each other.[4]

These policy aims express not only a broad array of concerns but also the spirit of merging and restructuring of the ends and means to more effective pursuit of solutions or improvements to urban living conditions. As part of this evolution toward contemporary urban growth policy, the growth-related objectives for the *Strategic Plan for the Southeast*, as endorsed by the Secretary of State for the Environment, offer more precise organisation for action against the policy concerns relevant to our evaluation, namely:

> ... to match population and employment growth, so far as this is practicable and consistent with expansion of the specialised role of Central London, taking advantage of opportunities to link the movement of workers with the further dispersal of employment opportunities;

> to promote the functional structuring of the Southeast into city regions relatively independent of London and thus allow for the development of efficient labour and employment markets for both employers and workers, without posing journey-to-work and congestion problems, and for the development of centres offering a wide range of community services;

> to provide ... for a wide variety of housing requirements and of job opportunities and for improved environmental standards in both new and existing urban areas, especially Inner London;

> to make the best use of the countryside, by protecting from urban

instrusion extensive areas of open country; ... which offer opportunities for open air recreation, ... of natural and historic heritage; and areas which separate and prevent the coalescence of urban settlements, thus helping to give them an identity and distinctive setting ... [5]

The objectives seem to recognise that policy implementation most likely must work and live with certain features of urban growth trends even while altering the results of the latter for purposes of socio-economic and environmental improvement.

The North American scene offers as much concern over policy issues but only the first inkling of implementation intent or likely strategies. One discovers, in the United States, a struggle between more vigorous initiatives desired in the federal legislature and a pronounced reticence in the federal executive to offer any initiative whatever. In 1970, the Congress passed legislation containing the founding authority for developing, if not fully implementing, a national policy of urban growth. The basic purposes are set forth as follows:

The Urban Growth and New Community Development Act of 1970 (Title VII of the Housing and Urban Development Act of 1970, P.L. 91–609) states that the Congressional purpose and policy are ' ... to provide for the development of a national urban growth policy.' Such policy, according to the Act, should contain provisions for the following major components:

(1)   patterns of urbanisation and economic development offering a range of alternative locations from large metropolitan areas through small urban regions;
(2)   economic strength of all locales — central cities, suburbs, small communities, and rural areas;
(3)   reversal of any migration and physical growth patterns that reinforce disparities among regions;
(4)   comprehensive treatment of poverty and employment problems which are associated with disorderly urbanisation and rural decline;
(5)   good housing for all the population;
(6)   definition of the Federal Government's role in existing communities and encouraging planned, large-scale urban and new community development;
(7)   stronger governmental institutions to ensure balanced urban growth and stabilisation; and
(8)   Federal programme co-ordination to encourage desirable urban

growth patterns, prudent natural resource use, and protection of the physical environment.[6]

We are confronted here with a broad range of goals and policy concerns that have little strategic focus or hint of implementational feasibility. The executive response by the Domestic Affairs Council, as required in the Act, was the first biennial report on national urban growth.[7] This document offered no unifying goal framework and, in fact, argued that a consistent and closely co-ordinated national policy was likely to be infeasible and undesirable. This impasse is reflected currently in the debates over special revenue sharing for urban development purposes which is revolving around the degrees of Federal guidelines or 'strings' to be attached to assert Federal policy directives.[8] Again, the legislature is in favour of rather more strings than the executive wishes to attach to the spending discretion of states and municipalities.

The numerous objectives for urban growth policy tend to resolve themselves along two basic lines: (1) greater growth mainly to produce more, or an adequate number of, jobs at constantly rising real incomes, which usually implies continuing improvement of industrial and commercial efficiency; and (2) greater equity of socio-economic and physical environmental sorts, which implies redistributions to income and jobs or occupational status, changes in residential and service activity locations, and geographic constraints on industrial and commercial sitings and on urbanisation in environmentally sensitive areas.

Some analytical constructs for policy development and assessment

The objectives require, in accordance with the realities of urban growth trends: (1) the clustering of some minimal concentration of industrial and commercial enterprise to generate private sector externalities; (2) the emergence of (a) a sufficiently large and varied labour market that permits a range of choice and likelihood of job replacement without residential removal, or migration from one area to another, and an adequate range of talents for employment in the basic (export) industries in all sectors, and (b) effective demand for the generation of rich variety in the non-basic (local service) industries; and (3) the concentration of adequate infrastructure to generate the public sector externalities, e.g. cultural/educational opportunities, recreational/physical amenity access, transport/communication accessibility within an urban area and to other urban centres, and housing with its attendant residential amenities.

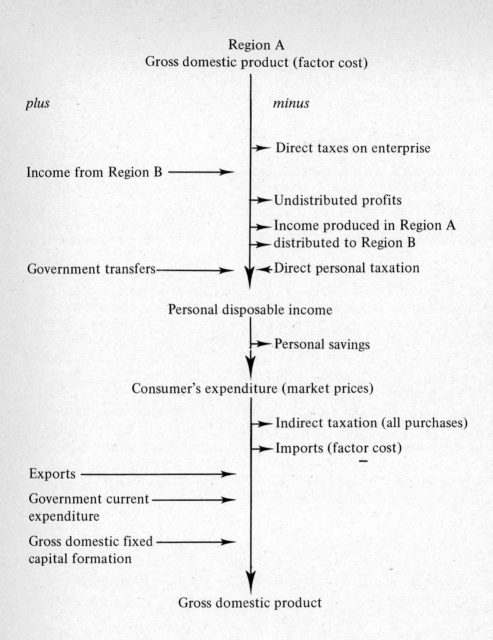

Region A
Gross domestic product (factor cost)

plus   *minus*

Direct taxes on enterprise

Income from Region B ⟶

Undistributed profits

Income produced in Region A
distributed to Region B

Government transfers ⟶ ⟵ Direct personal taxation

Personal disposable income

Personal savings

Consumer's expenditure (market prices)

Indirect taxation (all purchases)

Imports (factor cost)

Exports ⟶

Government current ⟶
expenditure

Gross domestic fixed ⟶
capital formation

Gross domestic product

Fig. 5.1 Example of multiplier leverage.

Source: D. B. Steele, 'A numbers game (or the return of regional multipliers)' *Regional Studies* vol. 6, no. 2, June 1972, p. 117.

When activity and population increments are initially subsidised into an urban area or larger region through use of public instruments, the leverage counted on to generate further growth or ultimately higher rates of growth emanates from various 'multiplier processes'. The typical model for such multiplier leverage, shown in Figure 5.1, indicates that the size and composition of resulting change, in this case measured by level of gross area product or output, is dependent on the amount of exogenous (independently determined) income and expenditure 'injections' into the area on the plus side, less the tax, saving, and import 'leakages' from the endogenous (dependent) income and spending steams generated within the area on the minus side. In the relatively open (high proportion of output entering into trade with other areas) economy of a geographically circumscribed urban area, the hypothesised most significant generators of new activity, income, and population are exports, the level and composition of which are established by demands and policies beyond the control of the locality itself. The size of any multiplier effect, and thereby the increase in total activity, income, and population attributable to given increments in export or basic activities, is dependent on the proportion of subsequent purchases between firms and public organisations and consumer purchases that are made within the confines of the locality. These proportions of successive rounds of spending are closely associated with the size and richness or variety of the local service sector itself; the larger in size and richness, the greater the likelihood of higher proportions of internal spending (less leakage) and the more multiplier leverage available to public subsidisation of growth in any given locale.

Regional economic promotion efforts have given greater attention to technical production linkages and attendant inter-industry purchasing pat-

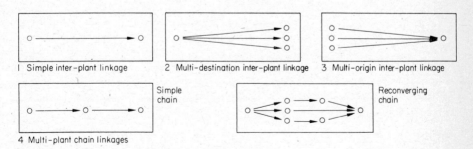

Fig. 5.2   Inter-plant linkage classification.

Source: C. W. Moore, 'Industrial linkage development paths in growth poles: a research methodology' *Environment and Planning* vol. 4, no. 3, 1972, p. 259.

terns in the hope of establishing growing complexes of exporting manufacturing activity and knots of local suppliers. These patterns of functional interdependency are complex and many combinations are possible, as seen from the diagrams of Figure 5.2. One quickly gets involved in chains that fan out, converge, or, after diffusing, reconverge again. The time and cost involved in obtaining data to test hypotheses of interaction and specify expected patterns make prediction of policy action difficult. In addition to these functional linkages, however, the spatial location implications have to be determined to say what plant location in a particular locality means in the way of future associated growth.

The inter-plant linkages in West Germany have held some surprises for regional policy implementers, as pointed out by the geographic purchase patterns identified in Table 5.1. If the planners are thinking in terms of integrated complexes within particular small or medium sized communities, then we can see that the larger number of purchases lie beyond the 30-kilometre radius, thus frustrating that hope. A fair number of purchases are made in adjacent areas within 100 kilometres; but many purchases, including important items such as investment goods, are made with great frequency elsewhere in the country or abroad.

To get at the broader implications for balanced growth potential, we need to discriminate further with respect to job creation capacity and occupational shifts between industries and sectors in terms of the location-

Table 5.1

Supply linkages in Nordrhein-Westfalen

Type of delivery	Number of surveyed plants receiving most of their deliveries from:			
	Within 30 km. radius	Within remaining 100 km. radius	Remainder of FRG	Abroad
Raw materials	23	78	45	19
Auxiliary materials	52	39	20	–
Parts and components	21	45	50	7
Investment goods	7	21	80	5
Total	103	183	195	31

Note: Included were the chamber of commerce districts of Aachen, Arnsberg, Dortmund, Remscheid, Solingen and Wuppertal.

Source: Günter Krumme, 'Regional policies in West Germany', Department of Geography, University of Washington, Seattle 1973, p. 55a.

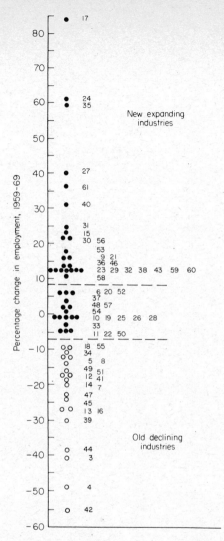

Fig. 5.3   Rates of employment change in Great Britain, 1959–69.

Source: W. F. Lever, 'Industrial movement, spatial association, and functional linkages' *Regional Studies* vol. 6, no. 4 December 1972, p. 380.

al needs and behaviour of the decision-making units, i.e. private and public agencies and institutions. The distinction between new and expanding activities and old and declining ones made in Figure 5.3 assists in sorting out paths of growth and clustering of activities. Expanding industries are those with a greater than 10 per cent employment rise over the decade, and declining industries are those with a greater than 5 per cent

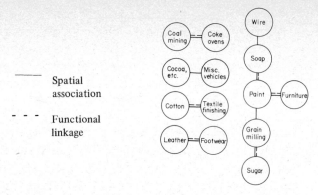

Fig. 5.4   Spatial association: old industries in Great Britain.

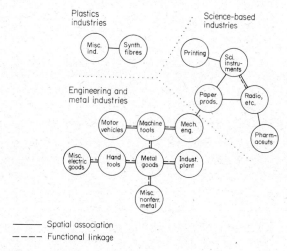

Fig. 5.5   Spatial association: new industries in Great Britain.
Source: Lever, ibid., pp. 381 and 382.

loss. Both functional and spatial linkages are markedly different between these two industry groups, as evidenced by comparison of their patterns in Figures 5.4 and 5.5. The old industries have firms linked in isolated pairs with unidirectional resource/processing connections. The only exceptions are port oriented activities that have reliance on bulky imported raw materials. By contrast, the new industries form into more complex inter-locking sets. The engineering and metal industries display an impressive set of paralell functional/spatial linkages producing concentration in the West Midlands conurbation of England. Of even greater interest are the location-al proclivities of the science-based expanding industries '... which are functionally unlinked but spatially concentrated very largely in the Greater London and Metropolitan regions, which have 23·8 per cent of Britain's total manufacturing labour force, but 58·3 per cent of employment in scientific instrument manufacture. 47·0 per cent of employment in printing, 46·9 per cent of employment in radio equipment, 44·4 per cent of employment in pharmaceuticals, ... '.[9]

The similarity of this latter pattern of spatially clustered activities to the earlier discussed case of New York City is evident. But the lack of identifiable functional links, when measured by input—output or purchase/sale relationships as was done here, calls for measurement of the contact interactions that better define the sphere of externalities generated for the sustenance of what are perhaps better described as being, to some extent, quaternary functions even though still categorised under the manufacturing label. The densely articulated web of such mutual dependencies is portrayed for Central London in Figure 5.6. We can now discern significant functional links representing more the flows of ideas and information necessary to fuel the sophisticated and efficient production processes of these sectors that adhere to the rich externality environments that have grown up in and around larger urban agglomerations. In this sense, we can say that these kinds of activities, which are often described as mobile or 'footloose', are tied to resource bases much as earlier secondary processing industries, but in this case the resource consists of man-built sources of supply, market destinations of service and specialised product outputs, and complex sets of private and public amenities.

The rate and the structure and quality of growth in the non-basic or service sector of a locality, hypothesised as being dependent on the generation of externally determined basic or export growth, is influenced profoundly by the level and pattern of so-called 'final demand' or local consumer expenditures of household units in addition to the aforementioned 'intermediate demand' levels and patterns between production units. We return now to the significance of changing occupational structures in urban areas and the expectations and tastes and preferences of upwardly mobile versus static populations. The pattern of first, second, and third-stage purchases of the products and services of different kinds of firms portrayed in Table 5.2 indicates the nature of potential demands on the local non-basic sector in the New York metropolitan area. When the employment structure in an area provides higher paying and educationally more demanding jobs we tend to find the effective demand of the active population and their families placing more pressure on the private sector for more and better goods and services and on the public sector for greater socio-economic and physical amenities. Households themselves become

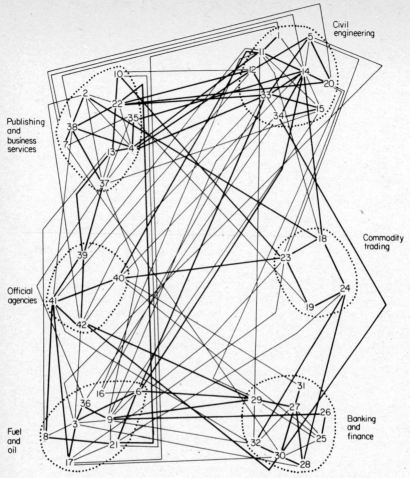

Fig. 5.6   Inter-sectoral contact flows and office clusters in Central London, 1973.

Notes: 1 Data are based on a sample survey of contacts between commercial offices in different business sectors.

2 Sectors are grouped into clusters on the basis of their pattern of linkages.

3 A heavy line indicates that both of the linked office sectors direct 50 per cent more contacts to each other than would be expected given their respected shares of all recorded contacts. A lighter line indicates a one-way relationship in the direction of the arrow.

Source: John B. Goddard, 'Information flows and the development of the urban system: theoretical considerations and policy implications', Paper prepared for the Urban Economics Conference of the Centre for Environmental Studies, 10–13 July 1973, University of Keele, England, p. 13.

84

Table 5.2

Sources of purchase for major industries in the New York SMSA

| Industry | Product type | Major purchasers | | | Durable/ non-durable |
		First	Second	Third	
Food	Consumer	*Households*	Food	Agriculture	Non-durable
Textiles	Industrial	Textile	Apparel	*Households*	Non-durable
Apparel	Consumer	*Households*	Apparel	Government	Non-durable
Printing	Industrial	Business	*Households*	Printing	Non-durable
Chemicals	Industrial	Chemical	*Households*	Textiles,	Durable
Fabricated metals	Industrial	Construction	Transportation	Fabricated metals	Durable
Machinery, non-elec.	Industrial	Capital	Non-elec. machinery	Government	Durable
Electric machinery	Industrial	*Households*	Elec. machinery	Capital	Durable
Misc. manufactures	Industrial	*Households*	Misc. manufactures	Capital	Durable

Source: Leone, op. cit., p. 181.

85

Table 5.3

Median growth rates of various types of economic areas, 1960—70

Economic area focuses upon:

Population size-class of economic area in 1970 (in thousands)	Centre of metropolitan status				Centre of less than metropolitan status						
	and sources of earnings of area was derived in 1967 from:										
	>12·5% Federal Government	>60% residentiary	Federal and residentiary	Diversified sources	>12·5% Federal Government	>60% residentiary	Federal and residentiary	Diversified sources	>25% agriculture	Federal and agriculture	>12·5% mining
1. 100 – 225	a	a	a	a	15·3	-2·05	b	8·6	-8·05	b	b
2. 225 – 500	b	1·7	23·7	-3·0	9·7	4·9	b	4·0	-4·0	-2·5	-4·6
3. 500 – 1,000	7·2	11·0	18·2	15·5	10·7	12·0	b	9·6	b	b	b
4. 1,000 – 2,250	27·2	18·9	15·4	11·8	9·6	b	11·7	9·0	b	b	b
5. 2,250 – 5,000	35·9	14·9	b	11·5	a	a	a	a	a	a	a
6. 5,000 – 10,000	b	12·7	b	b	a	a	a	a	a	a	a
7. 10,000 and over	b	11·1	b	b	a	a	a	a	a	a	a

Notes: a. No centres of this level.
b. No centres of this type.
National Growth Rate 1960—70 was 13·3 per cent.

Source: Berry, 'Contemporary Urbanization...', op. cit., p. 19.

more important primary, secondary, or other stage purchasers from both the basic and rising number of non-basic producers.

An interesting pattern of growth advantage emerges for daily urban systems in the United States when their growth rates are stratified by selected sources of demand as shown in Table 5.3. Searching for an explanation of the earlier-noted deviations from size-related growth trends, observed in Figure 4.6, we see now that ' ... the Federal Government or residentiary (non-basic) activities, or a combination of the two, were the principal sources of earnings in the rapid-growth economic areas of the 1960–1970 decade!'.[10] Over one-third of Federal payrolls and purchases from the private sector relate to high technology defence activities, atomic energy, space exploration, health research, and other higher scientific and related activities. The importance of large, high quality non-basic sectors, when combined with the governmentally generated basic activities, for achieving and maintaining high growth rates becomes apparent.

Major Federal defence and science expenditures are allocated to firms and individuals on the basis of ability to perform efficiently and meet the functional needs of those public sectors. It is not surprising then that we should discover a consistent bias in the kinds of areas favoured with defence and science contracts and locations of government facilities. When compared with the locational pattern of Federal expenditures that are explicitly or implicitly directed towards serving regionally differentiated needs, as is done in Table 5.4, we observe two complementary sets of expenditure incidence by types of areas in the United States. Concentration ratio values of one indicate that an area is receiving an expenditure share in proportion to its share of national population. Ratios higher or lower than one show, respectively, disproportionate concentration in or avoidance of areas. We find that, with small numbers of exceptions, defence and science expenditures are concentrated in the richest, fastest growing, large metropolitan, central-city, and suburban areas around the country. Conversely, we see 'regional' and 'mixed regional' expenditures concentrated in the poorest, slowest growing, non-metropolitan urban, rural, and regional assistance (EDA) designated areas. The areas of overlap between these two Federal categories of expenditure reside mainly in the richest and central-city areas. The types of regional expenditures found in the richest countries could be responding to environmental and public service upgrading demands. The highly qualified and paid commuter into the central city could account for that locus of defence and science expenditure.

Even in the abscence of a cohesive national urban growth policy in the United States, we can discern a distinct 'pattern of growth opportunity'

Table 5.4

Federal expenditure concentration ratios by functional categories for diverse types of areas in the United States, 1969/70

	Percentage of total outlays[a]	Poorest counties	Richest counties	Slowest growing counties[b]
Regional				
Agricultural programmes NEC	3·5	1·43	1·65	3·07
Natural resources	2·5	n.a.	n.a.	n.a.
Air transportation	0·5	0·18	1·62	0·45
Water transportation	0·5	0·11	4·28	3·54
Urban mass transit	*	0·00	4·37	3·37
Other ground transportation	2·4	1·37	0·64	1·25
Regional development	0·2	4·05	0·23	2·92
Housing and community aids	1·2	0·70	1·42	1·44
Air pollution control	*	n.a.	n.a.	n.a.
Water pollution control	0·1	n.a.	n.a.	n.a.
Business and farm economic opportunity loans	2·1	1·86	0·24	3·23
Regional development loans	0·4	3·71	0·13	2·85
Mixed regional				
Recreation	0·1	0·82	0·51	3·71
Business programmes	0·3	n.a.	n.a.	n.a.
Housing mortgage market	*	n.a.	n.a.	n.a.
Elementary and secondary education	1·2	1·52	0·65	1·14
Vocational education and manpower training	0·5	0·59	0·88	1·20
Other educational and manpower aids	0·4	n.a.	n.a.	n.a.
General government	1·6	n.a.	n.a.	n.a.
Housing loans	6·9	0·40	1·10	0·49
Defence and science				
Defence payrolls	10·5	0·18	0·68	0·43
Defence contracts	19·7	0·15	1·34	0·75
Defence-related act	*	n.a.	n.a.	n.a.
Atomic energy	1·3	0·80	2·23	0·80
Space research and technology	2·0	0·04	1·27	0·12
Health research	0·7	n.a.	n.a.	n.a.
Higher and science education	0·7	0·67	0·85	0·96

Notes: * Less than 0·1 per cent; [a] FY 1969; [b] All of these countries were declining in population; n.a. Not available.

Adapted from 'Locational analysis of federal expenditures in fiscal year 1969', mimeo, Evaluation Division, Office of Management and Budget, September 1970.

Concentration ratio = ratio of the share of expenditure to the population in that type of area. May be interpreted as a per capita relative share.

Faster growing counties	Metropolitan areas		Non-SMSA urban counties	Rural counties	Central cities	Suburbs	EDA counties
	>1,000,000	<1,000,000					
0·42	0·67	0·56	1·38	1·95	1·47	0·23	0·95
n.a.	n.a.	n.a.	n.a.	n.a.	n.a.	n.a.	n.a.
0·75	1·49	1·03	0·41	0·41	2·39	0·40	1·18
1·04	1·86	0·52	0·95	0·22	4·33	1·04	1·32
0·13	2·19	0·60	0·03	0·01	3·22	0·54	1·36
0·87	0·73	1·04	0·94	1·43	0·77	0·62	1·07
0·82	0·38	0·40	1·23	2·74	0·89	0·05	2·07
0·59	1·27	1·07	0·77	0·57	2·21	0·55	1·20
n.a.	n.a.	n.a.	n.a.	n.a.	n.a.	n.a.	n.a.
n.a.	n.a.	n.a.	n.a.	n.a.	n.a.	n.a.	n.a.
0·38	0·13	0·39	1·94	2·82	0·22	0·17	0·87
0·45	0·11	0·30	1·60	3·14	0·18	0·19	1·32
0·79	0·73	0·42	0·85	2·31	1·71	0·57	1·81
n.a.	n.a.	n.a.	n.a.	n.a.	n.a.	n.a.	n.a.
n.a.	n.a.	n.a.	n.a.	n.a.	n.a.	n.a.	n.a.
0·96	0·73	1·26	0·96	1·13	1·38	0·68	1·03
0·79	0·84	1·62	1·24	0·32	2·12	0·20	0·85
n.a.	n.a.	n.a.	n.a.	n.a.	n.a.	n.a.	n.a.
n.a.	n.a.	n.a.	n.a.	n.a.	n.a.	n.a.	n.a.
2·06	1·24	1·23	0·68	0·44	1·03	1·23	1·00
2·24	0·79	1·50	0·94	0·71	1·66	1·15	0·94
1·62	1·36	1·20	0·67	0·29	1·25	1·21	0·95
n.a.	n.a.	n.a.	n.a.	n.a.	n.a.	n.a.	n.a.
1·33	0·96	0·89	1·59	0·93	1·44	1·23	1·22
2·80	1·86	0·55	1·18	0·06	1·50	2·32	0·38
n.a.	n.a.	n.a.	n.a.	n.a.	n.a.	n.a.	n.a.
1·10	1·00	1·16	1·35	0·62	1·66	0·65	1·14

Source: William Alonso, 'Problems, purposes, and implicit policies for a national strategy of urbanization', Working Paper no. 158, Institute of Urban and Regional Development, University of California, Berkeley, August 1971, p. 15.

with which certain discriminatory forms of Federal expenditure are associated and to the furtherance of which they contribute. Conversely, we can
discern a 'pattern of non-growth compensation' traced out by the regional
expenditures but with little or no evidence of a contributory role in
shifting growth potentials toward such unfavoured areas.

Policy strategies aimed primarily at building up selected basic activities
in areas of stagnation or decline in the hope of extensive further multipli-
cation of growth miss the mark. The medium and longer-term potential
for self-sustaining growth, or dynamic replacement of activities in large
agglomerations where further elevation in absolute size is not desired,
resides in the man-made infrastructure and amenity of an area itself. As
Thompson has so succinctly put it:

> The local social overhead — the infrastructure — that has been amass-
> ed is, more than export diversification, the source of local vitality
> and endurance. Stable growth over short periods of time, say up to a
> decade, is largely a matter of the number of different current exports
> on which employment and income are based. But all products wax
> and wane, and so the long-range viability of any area must rest ulti-
> mately on its capacity to invent and/or innovate or otherwise acquire
> new export bases.
>
> The economic base of the larger metropolitan area is, then, the
> creativity of its universities and research parks, the sophistication of
> its engineering firms and financial institutions, the persuasiveness of
> its public relations and advertising agencies, the flexibility of its tran-
> sportation networks and utility systems, and all the other dimensions
> of infrastructure that facilitate the quick and orderly transfer from
> old dying bases to new growing ones. A diversified set of current
> exports — 'breadth' — softens the shock of exogenous change, while a
> rich infrastructure — 'depth' — facilitates the adjustment to change
> by providing the socio-economic institutions and physical facilities
> needed to initiate new enterprises, transfer capital from old to new
> forms, and retrain labour. [11]

Unless public policy instruments are joined and aimed toward building
independent growth or readjustment capability in desired locales, the current stream of regional economic assistance directed toward replacement
of specific disappearing jobs in problem regions can probably be projected
as far off into the future as anyone would care to forecast.

These externalities, signifying, as we have been arguing, independent
growth potential for urban areas, have specific significance for the well-
being and personal satisfaction of individuals and households as they mi-

Migratory motives

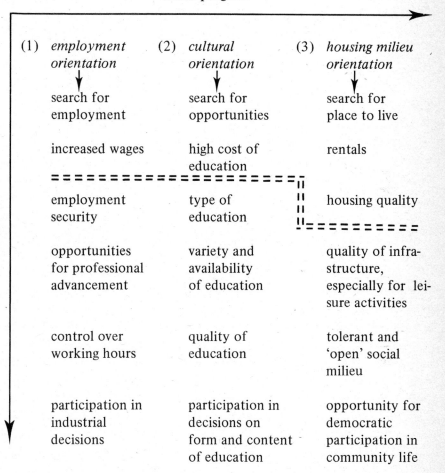

Fig. 5.7   How migratory motives change with social progress.

Source: Karl Ganser, 'Instruments for urban and regional development planning', mimeo, Conference on New Developments in Social and Regional Analysis, Bonn/Bad Godesberg, 6–9 August 1971, p. 31.

grate from one place to another or decide to remain in their original location. It is informative to match socio-economic advancement of individuals with their decisions to change living environments through migration from one kind of locality to another, as Ganser has done in the framework provided in Figure 5.7 to explain such adjustments occuring in West Germany. Social progress is seen as occurring down each column within given socio-economic levels; the most fundamental level being an employment orientation with greatest concern focused on improving working conditions, the intermediate level of cultural orientation being the transition to higher educational opportunity and the quantum leap from routine work to the more sophisticated milieu exemplifed by quaternary activities, and the highest level being one that reflects the growing concern and discretion shown toward their surroundings by those already earning higher incomes and enjoying greater leisure. Social progress across these orientations or levels is also shown with the implication of fairly systematic patterns of migration from smaller or declining areas to larger or expanding ones accompanying its realisation.

To the extent that 'social progress' can be reduced to discretionary choice in acquisition of material possessions, we have a strong indication from the index comparisons in Table 5.5 that the potential and ability (effective demand) for exercising such choice is progressively tied to employment and residence in larger and more complex urban environments. The index value for sparsely populated areas in Sweden is set at 100 and provides the base of comparison. There is no adjustment for living cost differentials, but from the results of Hoch's earlier noted real income comparisons we can infer likely sizeable increases in real consumption levels of the orders of magnitude depicted here.

In the broader schema of policy implementation strategies, we might envision a pattern of gains and losses to migrants and people residing in sending and receiving localities on the order of that depicted by Thompson in Figure 5.8. The path hypothesised to benefit all three groups of people is movement from rural areas and very small towns to medium or moderately large cities. A second stream of migration from small towns to very large metropolitan areas is seen to benefit only the migrants, whose personal incomes probably rise, ' ... but could leave everyone else worse off. Those left behind in the small town, growing smaller, face higher costs of utilities and higher taxes for those hard-to-contract (indivisible, heavy-fixed-cost) operations, and a reduced range of choice of goods, services and occupations. The big cities into which the migrants move may have little to gain from greater size but much to lose: increased congestion, greater trip distances, more political fragmentation and inner

Table 5.5

Consumption per member of household in regions at different levels of agglomeration in Sweden

	Metropolitan areas	Other city areas	Sparsely populated areas
Individual goods			
1 Food	116	102	100
2 Clothing	131	129	100
3 Household inventories	125	133	100
4 Liquor and tobacco	190	134	100
5 Housing	168	148	100
Total individual	137	123	100
6 Transportation	127	113	100
Semi-collective goods			
7 Private health and beauty	208	122	100
8 Amusements	163	144	100
9 Restaurants and processed food	223	161	100
10 Trips to other countries	377	227	100
Total semi-collective	199	151	100

Source: Åke E. Andersson, 'Regional economic policy – the Swedish experience', Göteborg Economic Institute, March 1973, p. 15.

city housing shortages'.[12] The following discussion of policy implementation strategies reflects approaches to dealing with dilemmas such as this which are inherent in urban growth guidance attempts.

Continued expansion or physical extension of urban agglomerations at lower densities accompanied by large daily movements of commuters across, as well as in and out of, the centres is rooted in complex sets of interacting socio-economic forces, a number of the more important of which are structured into the simplified model in Figure 5.9. We have attempted to chart the courses of change in a number of these factors that have relevance to the shifting emphasis in our study countries to development of urban growth strategies and the effective and beneficial use of

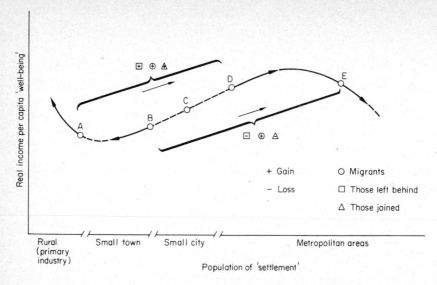

Fig. 5.8 Schematic representation of the relationship between the 'well-being' of migrants, those they leave behind and those they join, with special reference to the related size of the various populations.

Source: Wilbur R. Thompson, 'The national system of cities as an object of policy' *Urban Studies* vol. 9, no. 1, February 1972, p. 115.

policy instruments. The outcome of these interacting forces as graphed in this simple model, i.e. increasing separation of homes from workplaces, is manifested in geographical terms by increasing scale of urbanised areas but with continued primary and secondary concentrations of workplaces.

Sampling national policy responses: Great Britain, France, and the United States

Perhaps one of the best examples of strategy evolution aimed at dealing with the problems posed by continued urban expansion and the twin objectives of controlling the size and restructuring the internal components of the large agglomeration itself versus promotion of independent centres of growth, is found in the experience of policy implementation in the South East of England. This effort has evolved from the smaller first stage new towns encircling Greater London to the present restructuring of the region embodied in the *Strategic Plan for the Southeast.* [13]

The larger regional setting in which the strategy has been worked out is depicted in Figure 5.10. By our earlier definitions, the London urban area would encompass Greater London and most of the Metropolitan Region as it is mapped here. As the London agglomeration has expanded, the inner portion has maintained a significant degree of dominance as the employment centre for the region as shown by the surplus/deficit levels and values of job ratios for various portions of the South East in Table 5.6. Greater London had an excess of jobs over resident labour force of about 9 per cent in 1966, and the new towns had about a 7 per cent excess, while the remaining urbanised area surrounding London experienced a deficit of about 13 per cent. Inside the Green Belt, within Greater London itself, we can see further the great in-commuting potential remaining in the enormous job surplus of Central London and the surrounding deficits in the rest of the GLC territory shown by Figure 5.11. This employment surplus has not been eroded over the past 45 years and, in fact, rose by about 40 per cent between 1921 and 1966

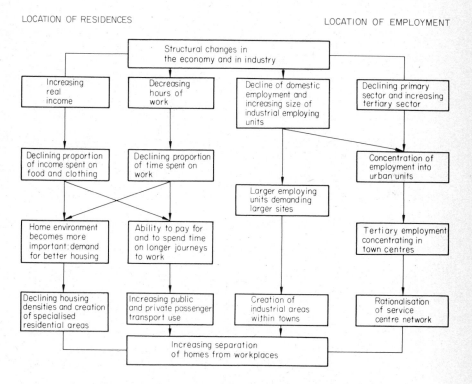

LOCATION OF RESIDENCES   LOCATION OF EMPLOYMENT

Fig. 5.9   The causes of increasing journey-to-work distances.

Source: A. M. Warnes, 'Estimates of journey-to-work distances from census statistics' *Regional Studies* vol. 6, no. 3, September 1972, p. 317.

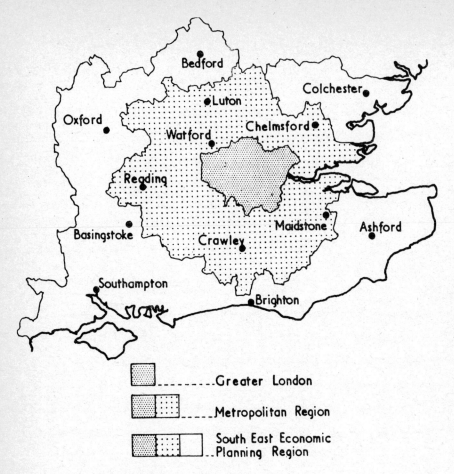

Fig. 5.10 South East Region in England.

Source: Town and Country Planning Association, *London Under Stress*, TCPA, London 1970, p. 7.

as seen from the figures in Table 5.7. The surplus was maintained by the decline in employed residents more than by the increase in numbers of jobs.

Because of the major planning objective of reducing the amount of commuting toward Central London and across the agglomeration, Thomas constructed indexes of commuting independence to measure the extent to which new town and other outlying employment centres were becoming relatively self-contained job market areas linking residence and workplace in addition to becoming simply job centres that were raising the level of longer distance cross-commuting within the agglomeration. The values of

Table 5.6

Employment imbalances in the London region in 1966

Area	Employment	Residents in employment (thousands)	Surplus or deficit	Job ratio (percentage)
Greater London Conurbation (GLC areas)	4,323	3,975	+348	109
London's new towns	213	200	+ 13	107
Remainder of Outer Metropolitan Area	1,817	2,085	−268	87
London region	6,353	6,260	+ 93	104

Source: Ray Thomas, *London's New Towns: A Study of Self-Contained and Balanced Communities*, PEP, London 1969, p. 414.

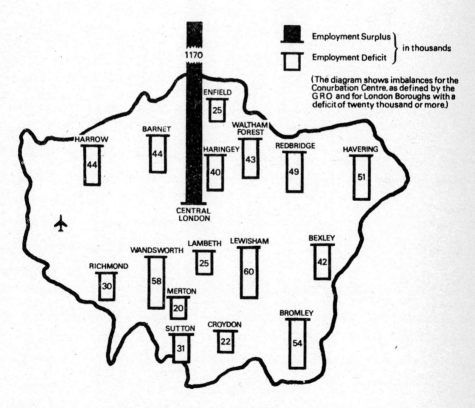

Fig. 5.11   Employment imbalances in London in 1966.

Source: Thomas, op. cit., p. 458.

Table 5.7

Employment and population in Central London, 1921–66

Year	Employment	Residents in employment (thousands)	Employment surplus
1921	1,175	325	850
1951	1,241	214	1,027
1961	1,296	194	1,102
1961	1,403	159	1,244
1966	1,340	140	1,200

Note: The figures for the period 1921–61 relate to the six former Metropolitan Boroughs of Finsbury, Holborn, St Marylebone, St Pancras and the City of London. The figures for 1961–66 relate to the conurbation centre as defined by the GRO.

Source: Thomas, op. cit., p. 459.

Table 5.8

Indices of commuting independence for London's new towns in 1951, 1961, and 1966

Town	1951	1961	1966
	(Ratio of local to crossing journeys)		
Harlow	1·42	2·04	2·05
Stevenage	0·92	2·29	2·03
Hemel Hempstead MB	1·31	1·82	1·72
Crawley	0·98	1·59	1·58
Welwyn Garden City	1·12	1·09	1·12
Bracknell	0·90	1·13	1·02
Basildon	0·36	0·96	0·96
Hatfield RD	0·65	0·63	0·66
Average (weighted)	0·85	1·33	1·33

Source: Thomas, op. cit., p. 393.

these 'independence indexes' are shown in Table 5.8 for London's new towns over the period from 1951 to 1966.

Local journeys are those of new town residents between home and work-place when both origin and destination are in a given town. Crossing journeys are those of residents to jobs outside their town of residence or of non-residents of a given town to workplaces in that town. The implications of local journeys becoming relatively more important, say constituting more than half of all home-to-work journeys (index values over one), include a presumed growth in richness of local service sectors and expanded employment opportunities and amenities for people not oriented to *daily* travel elsewhere in the London agglomeration.

The likelihood of attaining such independence or the feasibility of implementing such a strategy still cannot be disassociated from the relative locational and size attributes of the communities being evaluated. The degree of commuting independence has a moderately positive association with distance from Central London as shown by the array of places in Figure 5.12. A generally positive but rather dispersed pattern of associa-

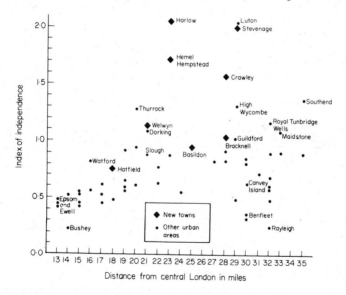

Fig. 5.12 Indices of commuting independence in S.E. England in 1966 by distance from Central London.

Note: The distance of an area from Central London is taken as the airline distance from Charing Cross to the approximate centre of the area in a whole number of miles.

Source: Thomas, ibid., pp. 404 and 406 (also applies to Fig. 5.13).

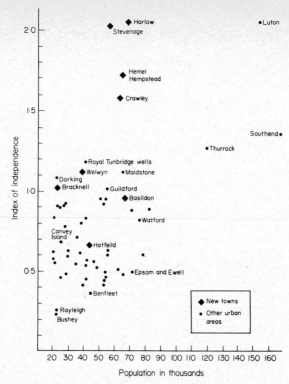

Fig. 5.13 Indices of commuting independence for towns within 35 miles of London by size.

tion is revealed in Figure 5.13 for the relationship between population size and independence index values. Further analysis is required to provide a more definitive explanation of why particular places have attained relatively higher levels of independence; these explanations may be rooted in such factors as qualities of commuting infrastructure linking given localities to London, thereby prolonging dormitory status for some as opposed to others.

When we look to see who it is that lives and works in these outlying centres as opposed to who commutes, we find an expected pattern, yet a somewhat hopeful one in terms of social balance objectives. Figure 5.14 charts the proportionate shares, on average for five new towns, of employed people making local, in, and out journeys by socio-economic group. Since the sizes of circles represent proportionate shares of total trips, we can perceive readily that skilled manual workers, junior non-manual workers, and semi-skilled manual workers constitute the bulk of all workers making all kinds of journeys. But, further, we can see that these groups plus the

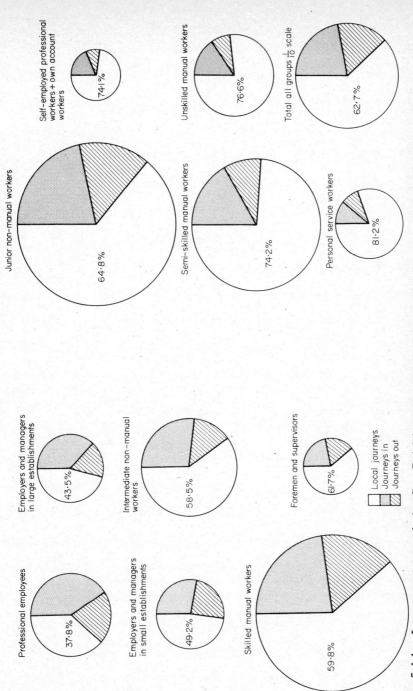

Fig. 5.14 Journeys to work in fire British new town areas in 1966 by socio-economic group.
Note: Areas of circles are proportional to total number of journeys in that group.
Source: Thomas, ibid., pp. 428 and 429.

101

unskilled and personal service workers each have by far the highest shares of local trips over all the socio-economic groups. The tertiary and quaternary types of workers, by contrast, show smaller shares of local trips and somewhat higher shares of journeys in, implying lower overall residence levels in the new towns for these groups. The self-employed professional and other trades workers, who constitute a relatively small proportion of total employment in any event, are the only exception to this pattern.

The implication of this pattern is that the tertiary–quaternary groups are having the least *combined* work and residentiary effects on these communities, while the other groups are having proportionately greater effects. However, one can draw a hopeful inference from the fairly significant combined shares of local and out journeys in the professional and managerial groups, indicating a reasonable base of such people who consider a new town as home and thereby have an interest in, and place demands on, the nature of growth in its non-basic sector.

A fundamental problem of past strategy implementation, of course, has been simply one of scale, viz. the job surplus of over a million for Central London (see Figure 5.11) as against the job surplus of 13,000 for all London's new towns (see Table 5.6). British policy has recognised this as reflected in the much higher designated sizes of second and third generation new towns, which are around the one-quarter million mark and which are being located at greater distances from London and the other conurbation centres. If this is the desired direction of policy evolution, then a continuing and systematic search for the promising centres of greatest future growth potential would provide a more effective basis for subsequent policy implementation. Policy- and decision-makers would then be wanting to consult 'growth maps' of Britain along the lines of that depicted in Figure 5.15 which identifies rapidly developing towns around England and Wales. Not only would pure balanced growth potential be a criterion for policy application, but also the relationship of these growth areas to other kinds of centres, such as the holiday and retirement areas identified in Figure 3.8, the latter having their own unique set of environmental amenity and public service requirements that could be impinged on seriously by intrusive general growth in adjacent localities.

The longer-term relevance of anticipating and guiding such growth potentials toward desirable societal ends is brought home in Figure 5.16, wherein the phenomenal growth path of Los Angeles pierces the fixed and static structure of the rank-size hierarchy in the United States over the 90-year period from 1860 to 1950, a period during which it rose from a rank of below 200 to fourth in the hierarchy. Under the facade of a stable urban hierarchy decade after decade, tremendous growth pressures and

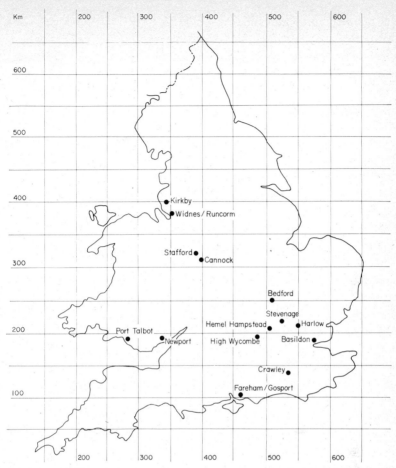

Fig. 5.15   Rapidly developing towns in England and Wales.

Source: Armen, op. cit., p. 173.

national redistributions of people and activities have occurred. In countries where urbanisation of rural populations is largely completed, including now the United States, most migrations are interurban exchanges, which may produce less massive and dramatic shifts between areas of a country. But, nonetheless, large migration streams continue to generate and accumulate socio-economic and environmental potentials and problems in specific areas.

Even though there exists no formally articulated national strategy for urban growth in Great Britain, there is a rather advanced concept of where growth ought not to occur, or should take place under highly restrictive conditions, based on criteria of conserving physical environmental amenity.

103

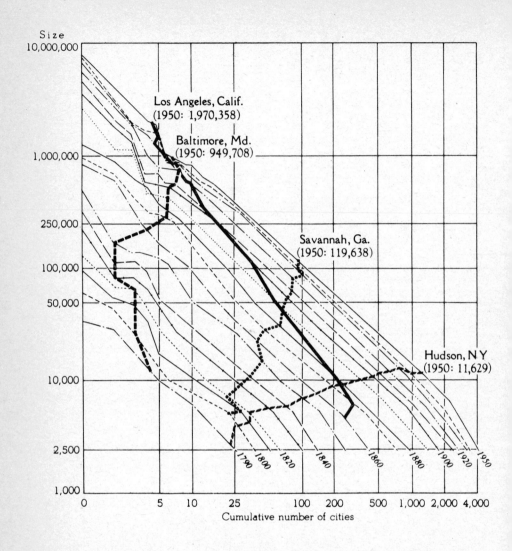

Fig. 5.16 Population of urbanised areas ranked by size, and change in rank of four selected cities in ranking of cumulative number of places by size in the United States, 1790–1950.

Source: Eric E. Lampart, 'The evolving system of cities in the United States, Urbanization and economic development' in *Issues in Urban Economics,* The Johns Hopkins Press, Baltimore 1968, p. 127.

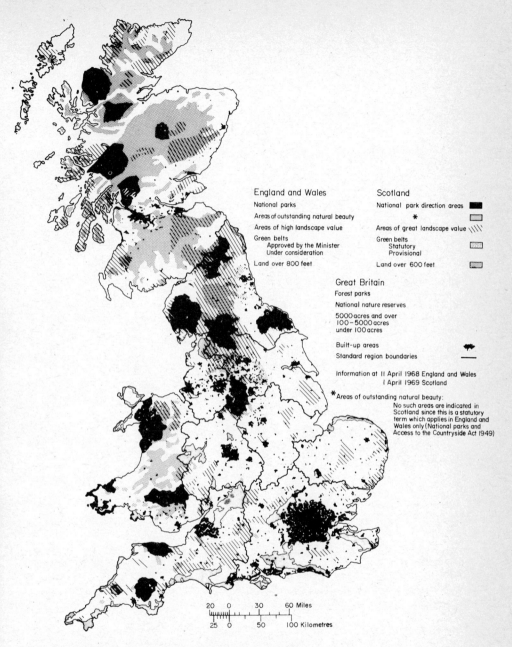

Fig. 5.17　Growth restraints in Great Britain.

Source: Department of the Environment, *Long Term Population,* op. cit., p. 54a. The map reproduced here is a black and white copy of an original in colour.

Table 5.9

Major restraints on development in Great Britain between 1966 and 1970, thousand acres

	England and Wales	Scotland (mainland)	Great Britain
Urban area 1970	4,330	565	4,895
Policy restraints – conservation areas			
National Parks	3,366	1,530	4,896
Forest Parks	167	262	429
National Nature Reserves	77	147	224
Areas of Outstanding Natural Beauty	2,746	–	2,746
Green Belts – statutory	1,211	333	3,989
– non-statutory	2,445		
Areas of High Landscape Value	5,974	5,160	11,134
Deduction for overlap of areas in the physical restraint category	−583	n.a.	n.a.
Total conservation areas	15,403	(7,432)	(23,418)
Physical restraint – high land			
Land over 800 feet not included in policy restraints category	1,246		
Land over 600 feet		9,840	
Deduction for overlap in policy restraints and physical restraints		−5,316	
Total actual and potential restraints	20,979	12,521	33,500
Total area	37,343	16,674	54,016

Source: Inter-departmental Study Group, *Long-Term Population Distribution in Great Britain – A Study*, HMSO and Department of the Environment, London 1971, p. 55.

The structure of this national system of protective growth restriction is mapped in Figure 5.17 and quantified in Table 5.9. Significant amounts of territory in Great Britain, then, are marked off for future non-growth or limited forms and types of activities. The extent and pattern of operation of this growth guiding and restraining system is shown by the percentages of land area under restraint or available for development in some degree (see Table 5.10 and Fig. 5.18). In terms of area already developed, under policy restraint, and available for future development, the different regions of Great Britain find themselves in greatly varying positions. Some of the reputedly pressured areas such as the South East and Midlands have 'balances' of between 40 and 75 per cent of total area remaining. Other areas of previous heavy industrialisation such as the Northern and North West regions have only about one-quarter of total area remaining in a developable balance category. Most of these variations arise from differences of proportions of land area placed under some classification of development restraint – anywhere from about 13 to 70 per cent for the various regions – rather than from large differences in proportions of land

Table 5.10

Distribution of urban area and policy restraints
on growth in Great Britain, 1966–70, by percentage of total area

Area	(1) Urban development, 1970	(2) Potential policy and physical restraints	(3) Total actual and potential restraints, (1) + (2)	(4) Balance: total area minus (3)
Northern	7·2	69·7	76·9	23·1
Yorkshire and				
Humberside	11·8	42·4	54·2	45·8
North West	26·1	47·1	73·2	26·8
East Midlands	11·5	13·3	24·8	75·2
West Midlands	13·5	40·3	53·8	46·2
East Anglia	7·1	27·3	34·4	65·6
South East	18·2	40·3	58·5	41·5
South West	8·1	51·9	60·0	40·0
England	12·4	43·6	56·0	44·0
Wales	6·7	50·6	57·3	42·7
England and Wales	11·6	44·6	56·2	43·8
Scotland (mainland)	3·4	71·7	75·1	24·9
Great Britain	9·1	53·0	62·0	38·0

Source: Ibid., p. 57.

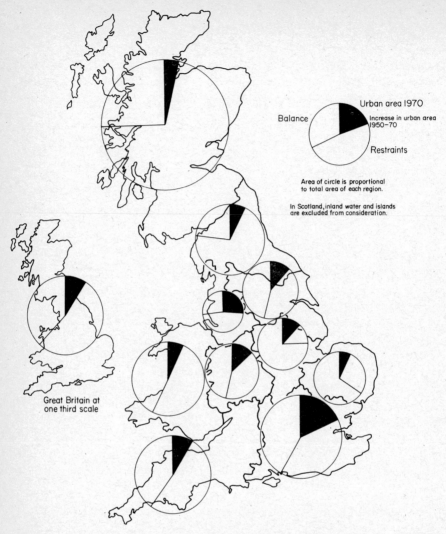

Fig. 5.18 Urbanisation in Great Britain. Regional distribution of urban land, recent increases and restraints to future development.

Source: Ibid., p. 60a.

under urban use – these are around 8 to 12 per cent for all regions except the North West and South East.

The most striking features of the figures and graphs of land distribution are the relatively large balances available for development and the relatively small proportions pre-empted for urban use up to the present time. One might note, however, the ominously large share of urban area that has fallen into that category in only the last 20 years. Scanning Figure 5.18, one gains a quick visual impression of generous amounts of developable area being available everywhere (save in three regions where the low balances are due more to high policy restraint levels than to high urbanisation levels), especially in congested areas such as the South East. Even with the very generous proportions of national territory under development restraint that we see here, many options remain for allocating growth to places of greatest potential, yet remain within the constrained pattern of urban non-intrusion displayed for Great Britain.

The need to rethink the reasons for maintaining very large amounts of open 'dead' or inactive space around and between urban areas has been raised as an issue by Peter Hall for the very reason of this great growth leverage emanating from the small quantities of land area, as proportions of national and regional totals, that are required relative to each new increment of urban growth occurring. As Hall points out, 'Robin Best had not yet demonstrated just how small a proportion of the total area of the country was covered by urban development (about 12 per cent of England and Wales now, and perhaps 17 or 18 per cent at most by the year 2000); nor had ... Gerald Wibberley, published his calculations of rising agricultural productivity and of the precise capitalised value per acre of the produce of farm land, which demonstrated how relatively little it mattered to preserve any but the best agricultural land'. [14]

The issue of effectively contributing to balanced urban growth, from the physical environmental amenity side, is broached most clearly in the Green Belt policies in Britain. They do represent, Hall remarks, 'a very significant chunk' of Great Britain — about 4 million acres or four-fifths of the already urbanised area of the country according to the figures in Table 5.9. What active and positive role does such built-environment restraint have on raising amenity and well-being levels in and around urban areas and agglomerations? The Green Belt around London, depicted in its most recent status by Figure 5.19, remains a source of controversy as a key to future livability in the central portion of England's South East. The older goals of agricultural preservation, from the days of Abercrombie, are argued by Hall and others to have become irrelevant without newer goals of active recreation use and natural environmental accessibility having been taken up adequately as reflected by the lack of park and sport facilities. The map of recreational and park facilities provided (see Figure 5.20) would reveal, as overlay to Figure 5.19, coincidence of many key facilities — picnic sites, country parks, and long distance paths — with the Green Belt area around London as of 1968. It would seem desirable to pursue vigorously the policy of appropriate active use of the Green Belt

Areas of outstanding natural beauty

Approved before 1968	--- Long distance paths
Approved after 1968	▲ Country parks
New Forest	● Picnic sites
	■ Indoor sports centres

Based on data supplied by the Countryside Commission and the Sports Council

Fig. 5.20 Major recreational facilities and Areas of Outstanding Natural Beauty in South East England, 1968.

Source: Ibid., p. 14a.

growth in the 'problem' regions by subsiding the latter everywhere that it seemed feasible to do so. The revised objectives of the Fifth Plan rejected minimisation of migration and more cogently aimed to: produce self-sustaining growth in all regions through selective development of the urban hierarchy by upgrading the relative size and status of 'intermediate' sized areas (the *métropoles d'équilibre*) and controlling the size and improving the form and structure of growth in the Paris region.

The present strategy of national urban growth policy implementation in France is one essentially of guiding public and private activities and popu-

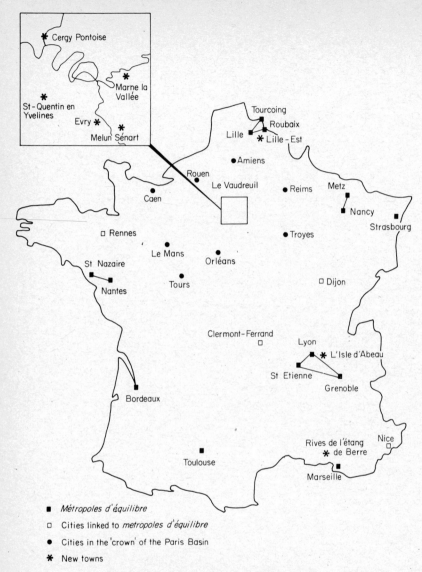

Fig. 5.21   Urban growth strategy map for France.

Source: DATAR, *Loi de finances 1973: aménagement du territoire,* Documentation française, Paris 1973, p. 61.

lation growth away from the Paris agglomeration and toward the *métropoles d'équilibre* plus the cities of the 'crown' encircling Paris in the Paris Basin. In addition, nine new towns have been designated — five in the Paris region, one near a city in the 'crown', and three in *métropoles* — to assist in growth promotion or internal restructuring within or adjacent to sizeable agglomerations. The geographical organisation of this strategy is mapped schematically in Figure 5.21. It is clear from this policy implementation view that French strategy fully recognises that the essence of assisting lagging areas and relieving congested or 'overdominant' ones resides in the leverage gained from providing alternative growth opportunities at the relevant scale in a variety of urban locales.

The geographical incidence of the implementational devices underlying the French strategy indicates further the recognition by policy- and decision-makers of feasibility requirements for redirecting growth in light of

Fig. 5.22   Distribution of support for tertiary sector activity in France.

Source: DATAR, *La Décentralisation du tertiaire. Les banques et les assurances,* Delegation à l'aménagement du territoire et a l'action regionale, Paris, June 1972, p. 11.

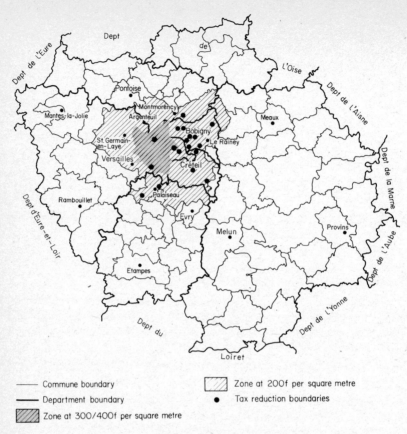

Fig. 5.23   Zones under the Paris Region office development tax.

Source: Ibid., p. 8.

existing trends. The map of tertiary sector (office and non-manufacturing) aid zones shown in Figure 5.22 allows assistance in all previous regional economic development areas plus concentration in key provincial cities whether or not the latter are in the older aid zones. The north-central part of the country is excluded from assistance, and, as we see in Figure 5.23, the inner portions of the Paris agglomeration purposely are burdened with a real estate development tax structure that penalises the centre the most with rate step-downs as one moves outward and with peripheral free centres to encourage suburban recentralisation, especially on the lagging east side of the agglomeration.

Emphasis on the tertiary (and by implication quaternary) sector in selected urban areas is a recent phenomenon in France and, as we shall see in our subsequent discussion of the use of policy instruments, the force and effect of this strategy are hard to assess at the present time. Nonetheless, based on earlier hypotheses about growth, the rising importance of service-sector jobs, and the potential benefits of an urban-centred strategy, the French reorientation of growth policy offers significant and promising innovation for more effective implementation.

The major land-use legislation recently introduced into the Congress in the United States [16] has already come under heavy criticism as being ineffective because the country still lacks a substantive urban growth strategy. One journalist observer of the controversy had noted that:

> Critics of the proposed land-use bills charge that it is virtually impossible to plan land use without first tackling the issue of growth. They say that to establish a planning programme without first establishing a growth policy is putting the cart before the horse, that a land-use plan should be a component of a larger growth policy encompassing native population growth and in-migration. [17]

The need for more effectively meeting these growth-rooted issues is becoming reflected as well in recent policy changes that are deemed necessary to carry out such programmes as those relating to environmental quality. To enforce the provisions of the Clean Air Act, the Environmental Protection Agency issued recently some very broad ranging regulations that state that:

> State or local agencies must have authority to prevent construction of facilities which would interfere with maintenance of the national standards because of their direct or indirect impact on air quality.
>
> States must identify areas where projected growth and development could result in violation of the national standards during the next ten years, and they must submit an analysis of such potential problems and plans for dealing with them.
>
> The analysis must deal with all significant air quality implications of growth and development, including additional air pollution from new commercial, industrial and residential development, and from increased demand for electricity and heat, from motor vehicle traffic, and from production of solid waste.
>
> This requirement was added to the regulations proposed on 18 April 1973, as a result of EPA's consideration of public comments suggesting that the regional air quality impact of generalised growth and development cannot adequately be assessed through individual source review procedures.

States will be required to identify potential problem areas within nine months and to submit their problem analyses and plans for maintaining the national standards within 24 months. [18]

These policy changes hardly comprise an urban growth policy, but they do imply the need for an over-arching guidance at the Federal level for reorientations of policy that are coming to be viewed not only as desirable but as progressively more irresistible for effective implementation of land-use and environmental quality policies and programmes.

Notes

[1] Bengt Thufvesson, 'Sweden's new regional planning legislation', OECD, U/ENV/73.9, Paris, April 1973, pp. 1 and 2.

[2] Based on conversation with Gösta Guteland of the Expert Group on Regional Affairs, Ministry of Labour and Housing, in Stockholm, 6 June 1973.

[3] Ir. Th. Quené, 'The Netherlands: both empty and crowded', Ministry of Housing and Physical Planning, The Hague, March 1968, pp. 14 and 17.

[4] F. W. Bone, 'United Kingdom national and regional policies affecting the location and distribution of urban growth', mimeo, Department of the Environment, London, no date, pp. 1 and 11.

[5] Monitoring Group, *Strategic Planning in the South east,* Department of the Environment, A First Report of the Monitoring Group, London, March 1973, p. 66.

[6] Philip H. Friedly, 'Urban growth and population distribution: research for future policy development' in *Planning 1971 - The Making of National Urban Growth Policy*, American Society of Planning Officials, Chicago 1971, pp. 79 and 80.

[7] Domestic Affairs Council, *Report on National Growth 1972*, Washington DC, United States GPO, 1972.

[8] The issues involved in revenue sharing are large and significant in the United States, but time and space do not permit their inclusion in this analysis and evaluation. Reasonable treatment would require an additional full-scale study. Some of the salient regional redistributional consequences of alternative schemes of income maintenace, categorical grants, general and special revenue sharing, and a value added tax, are analysed well in Stephen P. Dresch, 'Assessing the differential regional consequences of Federal tax-transfer policy', National Bureau of Economic Research, Inc., New York, April 1972.

⁹ W. F. Lever, 'Industrial movement, spatial association, and functional linkages', *Regional Studies* vol. 6, no. 4, December 1972, p. 380.

¹⁰ B. J. L. Berry, 'Contemporary urbanization processes', National Academy of Sciences, Washington DC, September 1971, p.12.

¹¹ Wilbur R. Thompson, 'Internal and external factors in the development of urban economies' in *Issues in Urban Economics*, The Johns Hopkins Press, Baltimore 1968, p. 53.

¹² Wilbur R. Thompson, 'The national system of cities as an object of policy' *Urban Studies* vol. 9, no. 1, February 1972, p. 115.

¹³ See the summary of this strategy and the most recent official assessment of its progress in: Monitoring Group, *Strategic Planning in the Southeast*, op.cit.

¹⁴ Peter Hall, 'Anatomy of the Green Belts' *New Society*, 4 January 1973, p. 12.

¹⁵ Hall, op.cit., p. 11.

¹⁶ The House and Senate Interior Committees are currently considering Bills to provide that each state establish a land-use planning process and, within five years, a land-use programme subject to Federal review.

¹⁷ Helen Leavitt, 'Land-use legislation: a toothless lion? ' *The Washington Star and Daily News*, Washington DC, Sunday, 3 June 1973.

¹⁸ United States Environmental Protection Agency, *Environmental News*, Washington DC, 11 June 1973.

PART III

Types and Use of Instruments: Examples of Innovation in Policy Implementation

6 Classification of the Range of Instruments Available

How can we conceive best the character and utility of the implementing tools available in our study countries for effecting strategies of urban growth and distribution such as those just evaluated? For our purposes, it is the responsiveness of public and private decisions pertaining to alternative urban locations of people and activity to policy actions that constitutes primary concern. Since most instruments produce results that contribute to economic, social, and environmental ends in varying degrees, we shall not define them accordingly as being 'economic instruments' or 'social instruments' but, rather, according to the degrees of directness or indirectness with which they affect location decisions as such. We are interested in the extent to which various instruments orient people and activities, whether by economic, social or administrative means, to different kinds of urban localities.

The desirable or undesirable 'side-effects' of different methods are of interest and may yield preferred emphases on particular kinds of instruments for reasons other than simple effectiveness for influencing location decisions. These side-effects may be noted in the arbitrariness or inequity with which certain groups of people or individuals are treated in the course of carrying out policies of growth and distribution under any given strategy that aims at larger social benefit on a national scale.

Generic types of policy instruments

The instruments with which we are dealing are those that exert primary effect on differentiating the growth potential and redistributing people and activities between growing and non-growing localities. Secondary and more remote levels of effect on growth and distribution can be observed or attributed to a very wide range of national governmental actions, most of which cannot be treated in this study because of time and space limitations. Such basic policy changes as that in the United States from categorical Federal grants to general and special revenue sharing, which places larger financial capability and decision-making discretion in the hands of lower governmental powers, deserve their own detailed evaluation. But unless particular Federal guides and requirements for growth policy implementation are being specified, there is little direct inference about growth strategy or effectiveness that can be drawn immediately from such a change in mode and governmental level of expenditure.

The more direct kinds of instruments are those that influence the location decisions of individually identified private and public decision-making entities — firms, persons or households, and agencies or institutions — and treat them in a differentiated manner depending on where they situate themselves geographically. Direct instrument applications would be exemplified by (1) subsidies or penalties for a particular firm on agreement that it locate or not locate plant or offices in one or more of a number of specified urban areas; (2) mobility and relocation allowances to workers and families for migrating to preferred places; and (3) government decision to relocate its own offices and facilities in accordance with public policy.

The more indirect kinds of instruments are those that primarily act to establish the general conditions for given levels and rates of growth in entire urban areas, and that influence in a diffuse or broad categorical manner the decisions of a whole universe of unidentified decision-makers who, in turn, constitute varying expected ranges of potential population and activities that could locate in alternative places. Indirect instrument applications would be exemplified by: (1) provision of general infrastructure (utilities and services) to induce a given rate and level of growth or accommodate a changing composition of population and activity in an area of constant size; and (2) large zones of controlled land use within or between areas wherein amenity resources (open space, intensive agriculture, recreation) complementary to dense built environments are generated.

The same instrument component, e.g. a new road link or communication capacity increase, could be viewed in one instance as a 'direct' instrument application when it is tied temporally and spatially to the development of an industrial estate or office centre and the particular private or public enterprises intending to locate there on condition of its provision. It could be viewed in another instance as an 'indirect' instrument application when provided as part of general infrastructure and not tied to the timing of a particular investment but intended to contribute to a desired level or accessibility to an entire community and any of the future activities that potentially might locate there.

The role of indirect instrument applications is primarily a longer run one redistributing general growth probabilities between urban areas by influencing the values of growth parameters such as relative accessibility (road and communication linkage with all other important urban areas) in such a way as to favour growth centres or accommodate shifting travel and communication demands in areas of non-growth. The role of direct instrument applications is primarily a shorter or more medium run one of either capitalising on existing feasible specific investment opportunities and subsidising them into reality or discouraging or preventing fruition in the context of the aforementioned existing and emerging general growth probabilities for different urban areas.

Along the time dimension of any implementation strategy, these direct and indirect instrument applications take on certain crucial requirements for interaction with one another. The 'hollow shell' of economic potential and social/environmental amenity fabricated from infrastructural investments requires 'filling-in' with what Hansen calls 'directly productive activities', i.e. the normal self-generating jobs of the private sector. As he puts it, '...private investment and investment in DPA [directly productive activities] are treated as synonymous. OC [overhead capital, or infrastructure in our usage], however, is divided into two components: social (SOC) and economic (EOC). Projects of the latter type are primarily oriented toward supporting DPA ... and include roads, bridges, harbours, power installations, and similar undertakings. ... SOC would include such activities as education, cultural projects, health programmes, and welfare'.[1] The presumption is that if infrastructural investments are employed actively as lead or simultaneous items to induce private and certain public (e.g. government defence facilities or procurement contracts) activities to locate as following items within a reasonable time frame, there is a need to ensure that the 'filling-in process' occur at an adequate pace. On the other hand, where infrastructure is being constrained in its level or rate of growth to maintain a relatively constant size in the total population and activity in an urban area, there is a need to ensure that the composition of infrastructural investment supports the pace of readjustment in private sectors where some may be in decline and need compensatory support (social or welfare services) and new activities may be on the rise requiring new levels and qualities of utilities and services not previously available (high speed rail or cable television).

Experience would seem to indicate that the direct instrument applications do indeed have a role complementary to indirect ones to play in guiding such activities as private and public office locations away from areas of 'over-concentration' and into suitable locales from the standpoints of growth potential and environmental criteria. Along the path of positive growth promotion for an area, one might envisage a temporal sequence in which commitment is first made to continuing reinforcement of higher growth probability through infrastructure investment, and then accompanied by direct inducement of private activities to ensure a full and timely response to the inter-area disequilibria set in motion by the indirect instruments. The inertia inherent in a stable system seem to imply that even if private and other 'directly productive activities' did respond eventually to indirectly established inter-area disequilibria, by changing migration direction or moving at all rather than staying put, those responses would begin to cumulate to sizeable proportions only long beyond the time horizon of the policy-makers unless a faster pace of change were to be underwritten by direct inducements to and controls on private locations.

In accordance with these definitional criteria, we identify major instruments categories as follows:

(1)　Direct government locations for its own account, e.g.:

(a)　locating offices and facilities;
(b)　locating contracts for procurement of goods and services;
(c)　locating state-owned enterprises.

(2)　Direct government controls on private-sector locations, e.g.:

(a)　office development permits and tax or other penalties;
(b)　manufacturing plant permits and tax or other penalties;
(c)　withholding of functionally required infrastructure.

(3)　Direct government inducements to private sector locations, e.g.:

(a)　capital, labour, and land subsidies to manufacturing and office developments – grants, low interest loans or guarantees, tax concessions, wage payments, site and building preparation;
(b)　advance provision of functionally required infrastructure;
(c)　mobility grants, allowances, and low interest loans to workers and families for travel and resettlement.

(4)　Indirect general infrastructure provision and location, e.g.:

(a)　utilities – transport/communication, water, fuel/energy, sanitation/waste disposal;
(b)　public services – education, recreation, culture, health, welfare.

(5)　Indirect land-use and location co-ordination, control, and regulation, e.g.:

(a)　use, density, intensity, and timing control zones;

124

(b)   co-ordinative bodies that apply guides and criteria to functional expenditures or financial arrangements and actions – interministerial committees, state/provincial or new town development corporations;
(c)   regulation of house rents, land prices, and the purchase, sale or use conditions of any other public or private product, service or activity.

Subsequent examples of actual instruments in use are drawn from the types most relevant to our discussions of innovation in instrument use under emerging and changing strategies of urban growth policy implementation. For this reason, some instruments, more heavily used under traditional regional economic growth policies, such as subsidies for manufacturing activity available indiscriminately across large problem regions, are not treated in any detail, if at all.[2]

Patterns of instrument use by type

The array of direct and indirect instruments in use by some of our selected countries, as shown in Table 6.1, displays an interesting pattern in existence a few years ago. There was an emphasis on direct capital and land subsidisation to industrial (mainly manufacturing) relocation, worker mobility subsidisation, and indirect inducement through infrastructural support of the utility or economic overhead variety (roads, energy, and so on). Much sparser support was available for moving enterprise from large urban areas to newer centres of growth, direct control of activity location, tying government activities or procurements to locational policies, or supplying infrastructural support of the service or social overhead variety (education, health, welfare, and so on). Virtually no indication was given of direct labour subsidation per worker employed in assisted localities.

Taking note of the issue raised by the last item, lack of labour subsidisation, criticism offered has argued that if the objective is job creation, even of just the manufacturing variety, a more effective way of raising the number of jobs *in the assisted areas* would be to pay a premium for each job brought forth by private enterprise. The capital subsidy, it is hypothesised, probably has reduced job potential in problem regions, thereby exacerbating unemployment in the latter and migration from them to congested areas. Andersson has observed in his evaluation of Swedish experience that:

> In 1965 the political catch word in regional policy was changed from 'men to jobs' into 'jobs to men'. The main means to get this new

Table 6.1

Central government measures in European countries

General	Industry	Labour	Type of measure	Fed. Rep. Germany	UK	France	Netherlands
A			Regional funds, societies for regional developments	×	×	×	
B			Improvements of regional infrastructure (roads, etc.)	×	×	×	×
C			Accompanying social measures				×
D			Decentralisation of public institutions			×	
E			Decentralisation into new towns		×		
F			Government orders	×			
G			Establishment licence or prohibition		×		

H	Subsidies on land and/or buildings	X	X		X
J	Subsidies on industrial equipment	X	X		X
K	Loans, if necessary, at a low rate of interest	X	X		X
L	State guarantees	X	X		X
M	State participation		X		
N	Reduction on transport rates	X			
O	Tax facilities	X	X		X
P	Exemption from import duty				
Q	Subsidies on the cost of training or retraining	X	X		X
R	Subsidies on the cost of moving	X	X		X

Source: Leo H. Klaassen, *Area Economic and Social Redevelopment*, OECD, Paris 1965, p. 63.

result was a capital subsidy scheme which after a first period of use 1965–1971 had the following structure [in Table 6.2].

Table 6.2

The structure of regional subsidies 1965–71 in Sweden

Type of subsidy	Proportion in total budget
Subsidies to local government expenditure	58 per cent
Subsidies to investment in private firms	36 per cent
Subsidies to education within private firms	5 per cent
Subsidies to local employment	1 per cent

After seven years of use of these mainly capital subsidising means in regional policy the result is highly disappointing. The regional variation in employment possibilties which was reduced during the period 1950–1965, *increased* in the period 1965–1970. The regional unemployment problem, which still is severe, is illustrated in the following table [Table 6.3].[3]

Table 6.3

Unemployment in total labour force for 1971 in different regions of Sweden

Stockholm metropolitan area	2·7 per cent
Göteborg and Malmö metropolitan areas	3·2 per cent
Local communities with a population of more than 90,000 inhabitants within 20 miles radius	4·0 per cent
Local communities with a population of 27,000 to 90,000 inhabitants within 20 miles radius and with more than 300,000 inhabitants within 60 miles radius	3·9 per cent
Local communities with less than 300,000 inhabitants within 60 miles radius	9·4 per cent
Less densely populated areas	11·2 per cent

In direct response to this kind of policy deficiency, the Regional Employment Premium was introduced in the United Kingdom. The regulations provide that:

The Regional Employment Premium is paid at the rates shown below in addition to the refund of Selective Employment Tax. The Regional Employment Premium is to be phased out over a period from September 1974.

Weekly rates of Regional Employment Premium

	Full-time employees	Part-time employees*
Men over 18	£1·5000	£0·7500
Women over 18 and boys	£0·7500	£0·3750
Girls	£0·4750	£0·2375

* Working less than 21 hours but more than eight hours weekly.

Broadly, any employer with a manufacturing establishment in a Special Development Area or a Development Area which is registered under Section 1 of the Selective Employment Payments Act 1966 qualifies for Regional Employment Premiums for his employees at that establishment. Firms engaged in scientific research or training related to manufacturing may also qualify.[4]

It can be seen from the proportionate cash value of total expenditure shown in Table 6.4 of inducement assistance available for enterprise in lagging areas, that this labour cost subsidy is still competing with sizeable capital underwriting by government. The capital assistance in Great Britain does have an administrative requirement attached to it, for use of government factories and interest subsidy and employer relocation grants, that 'sufficient additional employment' be generated to justify the assistance sought.[5] Even the extent of offset to more capital intensive enterprise in the Assisted Areas that can be offered by the employment premium is scheduled for elimination by the latter part of next year.

A more profound inadequacy of a policy revision such as the employment premium, against the nature and direction of our previously recounted growth trends and strategy reorientations, resides in its still being rooted in attempts at job-by-job replacement in largely manufacturing enterprise within large industrially declining areas. From a sectoral viewpoint, the attempt to encourage greater labour intensity in these industries may,

Table 6.4

Total cash value of investment incentive benefits
during the first three years of a project in respect of expenditure
for industrial buildings and machinery separately

Case	Expenditure on:	Industrial buildings (post-April 1972)	Machinery and plant
1	Non-assisted area	11·5	32·9
2	Intermediate area, no building grant	22·1	32·9
3	Intermediate area, 25 per cent building grant	41·6	32·9
4	Intermediate area, 35 per cent building grant	49·4	32·9
5	Development or special development area, no building grant	22·1	42·5
6	Development or special development area, 35 per cent building grant	49·4	42·5
7	Development area, 45 per cent building grant	57·1	42·5

Source: European Free Trade Association, *Industrial Mobility*, EFTA, Geneva, September 1971, p. 111.

in fact, frustrate their progress toward becoming competitively efficient. In this sense, these assisted or 'problem' areas really need to be able to provide the opportunities for shifts into the tertiary and quaternary occupations that are providing the main source of economic advancement in the healthier, faster-growing (although sometimes congested) urban areas. Otherwise, they face prospects of highly limited job potential within their own boundaries coupled with even more highly bounded upward socio-economic mobility for resident populations, save through migration out to locales where the action is located.

Recent revisions in French policy implementation under more explicit urban strategies tend to address the issue of balanced growth promotion in a more realistic and relevant fashion. Direct subsidisation for tertiary sector activities is provided for under the Decree of 11 April 1972, which modifies earlier industrial subsidy regulations by retaining some and adding new ones. Grants for office locations outside of Paris are available in the normal Regional Development Areas plus in all of the cities shown in Figure 5.21 whether the latter are in the regional aid areas or not. The grants are made to firms intending to: (1) create or decentralise their head offices, administration, and study or research services; (2) invest in any new tertiary activities; and (3) transfer any tertiary activities out of the Paris region. These grants, however, are not cumulable with the Regional Development Grant available to secondary-sector enterprise.

Minimal granting conditions require a funding of sufficient financial backing for the proposed enterprise and the creation of at least 100 permanent jobs (or 50 jobs if for head office or research facilities) in the new location. The normal time limit within which aid can be received to compensate for investment outlay is three years, but this may be extended to five if 300 or more jobs are being created.

The base used to calculate the percentage of investment expenditure eligible for the grants is expected not to exceed 50,000 francs per job; with ceilings on the proportions of total investment reimbursable set at: (1) 10 per cent for general administration and management locations; (2) 15 per cent for head offices and research; and (3) 20 per cent for transfer of head offices out of the Paris region. For projects of under 10 million francs, actual grants are not to exceed 15,000 francs per job created, but for projects over 10 million francs the ceiling per job can be overridden by 10 per cent but within the 20 per cent global reimbursement limit.[6]

This system of direct inducement to tertiary activities to locate in urban centres outside of the Paris region is applied in tandem with a pre-existing system of direct disincentives on tertiary locations within the Paris region that has been activated in very recent years. The decision-making heart of this office location control system, similar in many respects to that operating for the South East region in Great Britain, is the Decentralisation Committee. The functions and mode of operation of the Committee are described officially in the following manner:

1   *Role of the Committee*
    (1)   The main task of the Committee is the granting of permits in the Paris region; it ensures an intelligent application of the decentralisation policy of the government and helps to control the growth of the Paris region.
    (2)   The Committee also participates in the formulation of the government decentralisation policy (Article 13 of the 1967 Decree) in two main areas: definition of a public sector decentralisation policy, in particular administrations, the study of technical

and financial constraints which limit the areas in which this policy may be applied; in the private sector it analyses the possibilities of decentralisation in each branch of activity and the measures likely to favour decentralisation.

(3)   The Committee is also concerned with the location of activities both in the Paris region and in the rest of France in its role as adviser or in its permit-giving capacity. The clauses concerning location represent only one of the categories or reserve conditions according to which the Committee dispenses permits (Articles 9 and 11 of the Decree).

Regional planning on the national level is the fundamental task of DATAR. On the regional level the same can be said of the Prefecture of the Paris region. The Committee therefore is generally counselled by these two bodies with regard to location questions so that the location conditions demanded by the permit are in line with government policy on both the national and the regional level.

2   *Composition of the Committee*
Eight representatives of Ministers.
Two representatives of Prefects.
Two representatives from the administration in charge of the case under discussion.
Seven members named by the Prime Minister.

3   *Permit procedure*
(1)   *Rules*: Since 1955 any industrialist, administrative body or service desiring to create or develop an activity in the Paris region must obtain a permit, i.e. an administrative decision favouring his project. This decision fixes the developed floorspace that the demander may use. The permit is required for undertakings of a certain size. For the private sector the decision is taken at ministerial level [Minister of Public Works and Housing] on the advice of the Committee; for State Affairs the decision is taken by the Committee itself and only the Prime Minister has the right of appeal.

(2)   *Process*: The secretariat of the Committee is provided by the Ministry of Public Works and Housing. It receives the permit requests, ensures the addition by the parties concerned of all the necessary information for the Committee concerning the activities of the firm, then transmits the papers for each case to the members of the Committee, adding the case to the agenda for the next

meeting, which takes place twice a month, except in August. This comprises a meeting of the permanent section in the morning, followed by a full meeting of the Committee in the afternoon. Three members of the Committee play a special role and guide the proceedings by means of direct contact with the body making the request: the administration in charge of the economic aspects, DATAR for the regional policy aspect, and, failing the latter, the Prefecture of the Paris region for location in the Paris region.[7]

Construction permits are required for areas over 1,000 square metres and are accorded by the Committee to two kinds of applicants: (1) the speculative building promotor, building to sell or rent to other parties and whose office space is referred to as *bureaux en blanc*; and (2) the owner-occupant applicant building for his own predetermined use and whose office space is referred to as *bureaux affectés*.

Before offices can be occupied, another permit is required. In the case of the promotor-built offices, the permit is granted on the basis of the nature of the tertiary activity to be carried out on the premises when occupants subsequently have been identified. Since the activity of the applicant constructing for his own use is usually known in advance, permission to occupy is practically automatic. This two-stage permit system theoretically is intended to enable the French authorities to exercise greater and more precise control over the amount, location, and nature of tertiary activity in the Paris region.

There have been added recently two special tax burdens on office and other developers in various parts of the Paris region. These have the general intended effect of discouraging central locations and favouring both decentralisation to inner and outer suburban parts of the region (with special emphasis on creation of office centres to the east of the Ville de Paris) and dispersal to outside the region. The first special tax is a real estate development tax applied at time of initial construction. Until recently, this tax was applied at the uniform rate of 200 francs per square metre of space created over the whole of the Paris region. However, in 1971, a plan of geographically stratified and graduated rates was brought into operation to discourage firms from locating in Central Paris and the immediate western suburbs and favouring the outer areas of the region and the suburban poles on the pattern displayed in Figure 5.23 (see above). The rates are graduated in 100 franc increments from the nominal level of 100 francs per square metre in the most favoured zone to 400 francs per square metre in the most heavily penalised zone. The current maximum rate is likely to be raised to 500 francs per square metre in 1974, the largest increase possible without new legislative authority, in an attempt to make it a measurable proportion of the high and rising costs of office development. An even more sizeable burden is imposed on the transformation of residential quarters into offices; this type of change, having been subject to a tax of 700 francs per square metre until 1972, is now taxed at 1,500 francs per square metre.

The second special tax, a transportation tax, was brought into force by decree in August 1971 and consists of a 1·7 per cent impost on salaries paid by employers who employ more than nine persons. The proceeds are destined for subvention of the public transport systems in the Paris region, the costs of which are relatively higher than for comparable services provided in the other larger cities of France. The intention is to make the private business sector beneficiaries pay for maintaining good commuting access, at presumably higher relative costs, to a pool of high quality labour. There is also the equity question of avoiding an increase in transport system ticket prices, which is a sensitive public issue. It should be noted further that the proceeds of the real estate development tax are intended to be divided equally between assisting the financing of infrastructural improvements in the Paris region, on the one hand, and the decentralisation and dispersal subsidies for secondary and tertiary activities, on the other.

Clearly, these French policy revisions with new forms of instrument use constitute an impressive and relevant move toward what we could call feasible implementation strategies. There is an attempt to shift meaningful jobs in growing economic sectors that can offer a base for upward mobility potential in the areas into which they are introduced. In addition, the tendency for job relocation to become a process of urban reconcentration in alternative growth areas around the country that come to be identified more definitively as such, contributes to the ability for more systematic physical environmental planning that establishes areas for relief of growth pressure and maintenance of complementary non-urban amenity.

We can see from Table 6.5 that by 1971 Sweden and the United Kingdom had moved toward operating a more effective set of urban oriented instruments including: assisting worker mobility away from designated areas and into such areas; location of government establishments; preferential treatment in the award of government contracts; transport and other public service concessions; and controls on private-sector firm locations. Serious emphasis on tertiary and quaternary functions, except in government office relocations, and clear mention of any kind of urban as opposed to regional strategy are absent. Selected concise evaluation of

Table 6.5

Current industrial mobility measures
in Sweden and the United Kingdom, 1971

Incentives and regional measures	Sweden	UK
Tax concessions	C	C
Tax concessions on investment	C	C
Loans available	C	C + L
Loans at subsidised interest	C + L	C + L
Loans granted	(C)	
Grants on industrial buildings	C	C
Grants on plant and machinery		V
Grants towards settling-in costs	(C)	C
Grants towards working capital		(C)
Grants towards labour costs	C	C
Grants on research and development	(L)	
Shareholding		(C)
Labour training aids	C	C
Financial aids to worker mobility away from designated areas	C	
Financial aids to worker mobility into designated areas	C	C
Industrial estates		C + L
Advance factories	V	C + L
Factory building for specific firms		C + L
Extra aid in providing industrial services	(C)	C + L
Location of government establishments	C	C
Preferential treatment in the award of government contracts	(C)	C
Transport and other public service concessions	C	
Building controls for industrial mobility purposes	(C)	C
Growth centre policy	L	

C = Operated by the central authorities.
L = Operated by the local (or regional) authorities.
V = Used but now discontinued.
(C), (L) = Available or operated but not particularly important.

Source: EFTA, *Industrial Mobility...*, op. cit., p. 56.

Table 6.6
Selected Federal programmes of possible assistance for new community growth and public facilities, in the United States, 1967

Programme	Administering agency	Eligible recipient
New community mortgage insurance for land acquisition and development – Title X.	HUD	Private developers.
Planning assistance grants: Urban planning assistance.	HUD	Cities (less than 50,000); counties; State, regional, and metropolitan planning agencies
Advances for public works planning.	HUD	Any non-Federal public agency.
Water and sewer facilities: Basic water and sewer facilities programme.	HUD	Local public body or agency, non-profit private corporation serving community under 10,000.
Waste treatment works construction.	Federal Water Pollution Administration, Department of Interior.	Any State, municipal or other public body.
Rural water and sewer systems.	Department of Agriculture.	Public and non-profit agencies in rural areas.
Advance acquisition of land.	HUD	Local public bodies or agencies.
Public facility loans.	HUD	Any local agency in a municipality under 50,000; designated development areas up to 150,000.
Urban mass transportation demonstration grants.	HUD	State, interstate, regional, or local public bodies.
Outdoor recreation assistance.	Department of the Interior.	States and through their local governments.

Loans	Loan guarantees	Grants	Technical assistance	Description
				Kind of assistance / Description

Loans	Loan guarantees	Grants	Technical assistance	Description
	X			Large-scale developments and new community land development costs including financing of public facilities; mortgage insurance extended to 30 years.
		X	X	Grants for comprehensive urban development planning programmes.
		X	X	Interest-free advances to plan public works and community facilities.
		X		50 per cent of the cost of land and construction of new water and sewer facilities.
		X		30 per cent of the cost of waste treatment works, including intercepting of outfall sewers; 40 per cent if State contributes at least 30 per cent, 50 per cent if State contributes 25 per cent, and project conforms with water quality standards. Grant increased by 10 per cent, if project conforms with comprehensive metropolitan plan.
X		X		Loans (10 per cent) and grants for development and construction costs of water or waste disposal systems.
		X		Grants for interest charges on funds borrowed to purchase land up to five years in advance of construction of public works and facilities.
X				Long-term construction loans (up to 40 years) for all types of public facilities where such credit is not otherwise available on reasonable terms.
			X	Grants ($\frac{2}{3}$ of cost) to test and demonstrate new ideas and methods for improving mass transportation systems and service.
		X		50 per cent matching grants for land acquisition or purchase of easements for outdoor recreation areas and facilities.

Table 6.6, continued

Programme	Administering agency	Eligible recipient
Airport development.	Federal Aviation Administration.	State and local public bodies.
Neighbourhood facilities.	HUD	Public bodies or agencies.
Educational facilities construction.	HUD	Public and private colleges and universities.
Adult basic education.	HUD	State educational agencies.
Areawide health facility planning.	HUD	State Hill–Burton agencies or other public or non-profit agencies through such State agencies.
Community mental health centres.	HUD	State, local public agencies and non-profit organisations.
Federal surplus real property.	General Services Administration.	State and local public agencies.
Small business financial assistance.	Small Business Administration.	Small independently owned and operated business.
Federal regional programmes: (a) Supplemental grants for Appalachia.	Department of Commerce.	Appalachian communities.
Public works and economic development.	Department of Commerce.	State and local agencies, private non-profit agencies.

Source: Advisory Commission on Intergovernmental Relations, *Urban and Rural America: Policies for Future Growth*, USGPO, Washington DC, April 1968, pp. 94 and 95.

Kind of assistance				Description
Loans	Loan guarantees	Grants	Technical assistance	
		X		50 per cent grants for planning acquisition and development of public airports.
		X	X	Grants to establish multipurpose neighbourhood centres for health, recreational, and social services. Grants cover $\frac{2}{3}$ of development costs $-\frac{3}{4}$ of cost in redevelopment areas under sec. 401, Public Works and Economic Act, 1965.
X		X		Grants and loans to assist recipients in financing the construction of facilities needed to expand their enrolment including extension programmes.
		X		Grants for support of instruction programmes below college level to persons 18 years or more who have not achieved a high school education.
		X		50 per cent grants of project costs to support areawide health facility planning and 75 per cent grants in developing comprehensive plans for co-ordination of health services.
		X		$\frac{1}{3}$ to $\frac{2}{3}$ grants to finance construction and staffing of mental health centres.
				Surplus property conveyed to State and local governments for park, recreation, airport, health or educational purposes.
X				Loans for construction, purchase of equipment, and for working capital for business conversion or expansion.
X		X		Supplementary grants up to 80 per cent of project costs of all Federal grant-in-aid programmes, including airports, vocational education, schools, hospitals, recreation, sewer and water systems and facilities, etc.
X		X		Grants up to 50 per cent of project costs and loans up to 100 per cent of land acquisition and improvements for public works and service facilities to encourage industrial or commercial expansion. Only projects in designated 'redevelopment areas' eligible.

recent use experience across most of these instruments is offered in the following sections of our study.

Even in a country such as the United States which lacks central national urban policy and strategy, an impressive array of general infrastructural assistance is available in the Federal armoury as shown by Table 6.6, but presently allocated without co-ordinated or consistent urban growth implications. One could imagine beneficially organising the locations of such infrastructure in a manner like that indicated in Table 6.7, for example, in order to establish growth patterns and size potentials for urban areas that better serve the varied needs of their populations. As noted earlier, in the United States not even first steps have yet been taken to come to grips with the complex problems of co-ordinating such assistance under a unified set of policies aimed toward beneficial forms of urban growth. Also as noted earlier, even the development of a unified set of policies is mired down in the impasse over revenue sharing.

The task of organising the co-ordination of diverse instrumentalities for implementation of a complex set of interlocking policies is, from the standpoints of both bureaucratic manageability and resolution of political conflict and interest group divergency, by far the most demanding requirement for the establishment of a national policy that could make any pretence to be operational and effective. That group of indirect instruments dealing with general land use and activity location co-ordination, control and regulation (instrument group number five in our earlier categorisation) comprises a key set of 'instrument organisers'. In other words, they themselves constitute primarily administrative instruments to facilitate and guide the application of combinations of other direct and indirect instruments when incompatibilities are to be avoided and synergistic effects are to be sought through congruence of functional, spatial, and temporal incidence.

Probably the least amount of innovative activity has occurred for urban growth policy implementation purposes in this latter instrument group although the need for it is great. We find complex decision and implementation processes existing even in the smaller countries with unitary governmental systems, such as the interactions between decisions at various governmental levels and the financial and location determinations for various major infrastructural items in Sweden as charted in Figure 6.1. The Riksdag, ministry and board designations indicate decisions and actions taken at the central government level, while county and local councils, or administrations, refer to provincial and municipal level decisions. In some areas, e.g. hospital construction, the finance and location decisions are fairly evenly shared between central and local authorities. But even where

Table 6.7

Classification of regional centres by amenities

Category of amenity	Centre of first order	Centre of second order	Centre of third order
1 Education	University with one or more facilities	More than one secondary school with at least one Latin school	One secondary school
2 Medical care	Hospital or hospitals with more than 700 beds	Hospital or hospitals with a total of 300–700 beds	Hospital or hospitals with a total of 50–300 beds
3 Social and cultural amenities	1 Sports stadium 2 Indoor swimming pool 3 Three cinemas with at least 25 performances a week 4 Theatre 5 Daily newspaper	Three or four of the five amenities listed	One or two of the five amenities listed
4 Regional government office	1 Employment office 2 District attorney 3 Tax-inspection 4 Chamber of commerce 5 Office of Federal police Four or five of these offices present	Two or three of the offices present	One of the offices present
5 Trade and traffic	1 Market or markets 2 Department stores 3 Banks 4 Regional bus centre 5 Specialised shops	Ranks according to a system of points attributed to the different institutions	

Source: Klaassen, op. cit., p. 91.

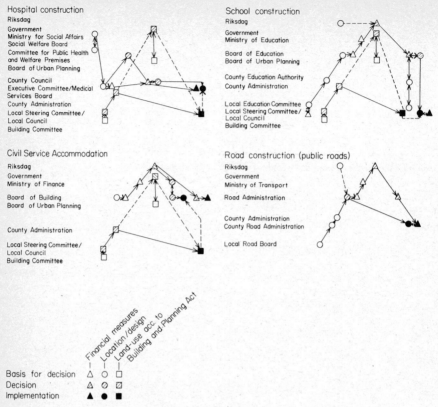

Fig. 6.1 Infrastructure desisions in Sweden.

Source: Odmann and Dahlberg, op. cit., p. 113.

such decisions rest more securely in central government hands, there is obvious need for co-ordination across the functional infrastructure categories, each of which has its own line of authority and implementation.

The Netherlands has approached more aggressively than most of our selected countries the task of establishing an operating mechanism to guide the diverse decisions on general infrastructure toward the flexible but unified ends of their urban growth and settlement policies. The overall co-ordinating environment for directing infrastructure decisions nationally is shown in Figure 6.2. The Cabinet Committee on Physical Planning brings all the relevant ministries together to discuss the higher policy issues revolving around important interactions — mutually supportive and conflicting ones. The National Physical Planning Committee is a working level group that considers in greater detail the co-ordinative paths that need to be followed by the various functional ministries. This type of

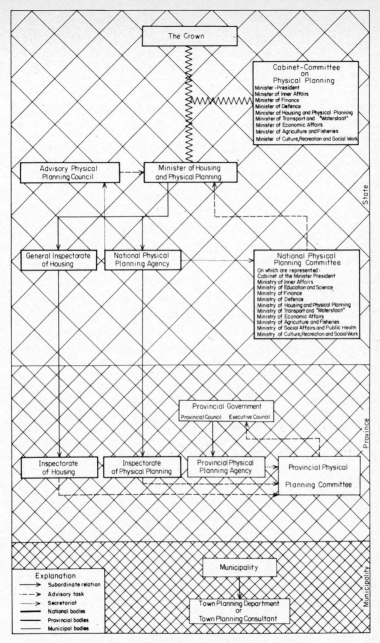

Fig. 6.2   Infrastructure co-ordination in the Netherlands.

Source: Ministry of Housing and Physical Planning, 'The organization of physical planning in the Netherlands', Ministry Information Service, the Hague 1970, p. 15.

co-ordination is intended to address the substantive issues across the three 'facets' of (1) physical planning, (2) economic planning, and (3) social planning, as these latter are conducted for and affect any one of the 14 or so 'public sectors' (functional ministries).[8]

Deriving from these co-ordinative arrangements, are the long-term 'structure schemes' prepared for the various major infrastructural categories. Prior to 1966 the co-ordination between the central government ministries was not strong. But since then the Ministry of Housing and Physical Planning, under the aegis of the framework just described and graphed in Figure 6.2, has established 'structure scheme committees' which prepare detailed policy guidance studies and reports for government decision. Reports on highways, electric power plant sitings and interconnecting transmission lines, and housing are in progress or completed. The presiding officers of these committees are people from outside government service to insure a degree of objectivity. The Physical Planning Service, in its role as secretariat to the interministry committee, places the final versions of these scheme reports before the committee for its consideration and approval. Any finally adopted structure schemes by the government and parliament would establish policy application guidelines and would be intended to serve as data for the more detailed provincial and local level planning and location decisions.

In order to provide specific focus on instrument use in the furtherance of policies for urban growth, we delve next into selected concise accounts of use experience. These exemplify the central nature of policy innovation in this field and cover a sampling of important direct and indirect forms of instrument application. We begin with evaluation of the more amorphous problems of general indirect infrastructure guidance and co-ordinative efforts and then move to examples of direct private and public activity inducement and control efforts in the tertiary and quaternary sectors.

Notes

[1] Niles M. Hansen, *French Regional Planning*, Edinburgh University Press, Edinburgh 1968, pp. 9 and 10.

[2] Detailed analysis and evaluation of the traditional instruments for regional growth promotion and the shifting emphasis to urban forms of such assistance are included in: Harry W. Richardson, 'The effectiveness of policy instruments to encourage the growth of small and medium-sized cities', Centre for Research in the Social Sciences, University of Kent at Canterbury, Canterbury, July 1973.

[3] Andersson, op.cit., p. 3.

[4] Department of Trade and Industry, *Incentives for Industry in the Assisted Areas*, HMSO, London 1972, p. 17.

[5] Ibid., p. 7.

[6] DATAR, *La Decentralisation du Tertiaire*, Délégation à l'aménagement du territoire et à l'action régionale, Paris 1972, pp. 15 and 16.

[7] Ibid., p. 14.

[8] This structuring was explained during a personal interview in The Hague with Mr Jan L. M. Kits Nieuwenkamp of the National Physical Planning Service.

7 Infrastructure Guidance and Control

One would, most likely, search in vain for an adequate example of consistent national strategic application of the full range of infrastructure − utilities and services − over time periods sufficient for evaluation of results aimed at serving growth promotion or containment in given types of areas. Even to find such consistent application for one or a few infrastructural items is something of a struggle. The reasons probably are clear enough: infrastructure serves diverse needs, its provision is bargained for from diverse public and private sources, and only recently have national governments and their constituents perceived strongly enough the possible desirability of co-ordinating its provision with growth and environmental quality objectives.

Transport in Greater London

The case of road transport infrastructure provision for Greater London, however, does provide a unique opportunity for evaluating the consequences of indirect instrument application serving to reduce overall growth potential in an already congested agglomeration perceived, by some, to be too large. Other, direct, instruments have been used to maintain something of a lid on Greater London growth and simultaneously siphon off activities for the Assisted Areas, e.g. industrial development certificates (IDCs) and office developments permits (ODPs). It could be argued persuasively enough that no containment policy should be inferred from the cautious provision of road and other auto-serving infrastructure in Greater London because no explicit policy guides exist linking it with growth potential reduction.

Nonetheless, the criteria established over time for not mindlessly accommodating ever higher levels of automobile usage, the demands and pressures for which have grown considerably since the Second World War, often relate to maintaining the present livability and amenity of London with roughly its present population level. We need not, in any event, claim explicit growth policy service, because the inferred effectiveness of constraining the level of automobile accessibility within Greater London has made it a *de facto* partner with the direct constraints, the Green Belt, and the new town policies in keeping agglomeration size below what it otherwise might have been. For this reason, automobile accessibility policy for Greater London provides one of those rare entry points for evaluating indirect instrument use having fairly precise implications for growth management.

Even in this case, there has been some inconsistency between central government and London local authority policies towards automobile-related transport infrastructure. The starting point for Greater London road planning is the set of connection places to the national road network converging on London. With regard to such national/local compatibility, the Greater London Development Plan (GLDP) states that:

Future primary roads in London must be planned in relationship to existing high capacity roads and the national motorway system.... There are two significant non-radial elements of the existing road plan.... The remaining elements of the existing system are radial roads arising from the historical position of London in the national transport system, *which has been reinforced in the last ten years* by the national motorway system.[1] [Author's italics]

The national highway planning that has helped to maintain London's pre-eminence produces a set of primary roads and motorways entering the area as depicted in Figure 7.1. Though the North Circular Road connects six of these main entering arteries, the remaining seven are left 'dangling' in this agglomeration of seven or eight million people. Completion of the circumnavigational road system has been the subject of heightened controversy on the local scene. The newly elected Labour Council for Greater London has just rejected the previously approved plans to complete this 'motorway box' in London and plans, once again, to view the alternatives afresh.

One need only look at the primary road networks for other major cities in Figure 7.2 to see the relatively underdeveloped state of the London network. Washington's beltway, Paris' peripherique, and Boston's and Chicago's multi radials show some European and most American cities to have committed themselves to significantly higher levels of internal auto access and thereby greater growth pressures and continuous spread of peripheral development. The comparisons of primary road mileage per thousand population shown in Table 7.1 reveal London to be rather below the levels of most other English agglomerations. Even more pertinently, the international comparisons of proposed miles of primary roads per

148

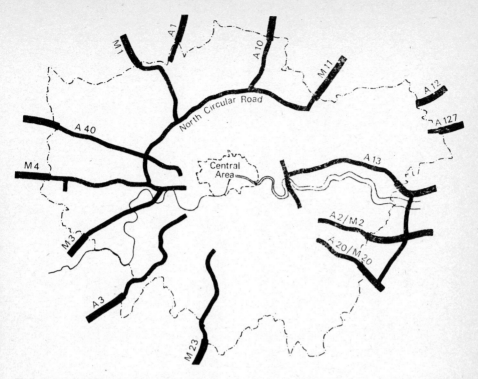

Fig. 7.1   Existing and committed primary roads and motorways in Greater London, 1970.

Source: Greater London Council, *Greater London Development Plan, Public Inquiry Proof,* E. 12.1, 'Transport', London, November 1970, p. 96.

million population shown in Table 7.2 point up the intention in Greater London to provide considerably less auto access in the future within its confines.

In accordance with these relatively lower levels of road provision, we find that the proportion of land consumed in the service of auto mobility is low also as shown by the comparisons in Table 7.3. In the same city size class, New York has an astonishing three times as much of its land area in road use as does London. In contrast to the American cities, London and the European examples in general seem still to have available other ameni-ty options than merely higher accessibility. From the proposed proportion of 12·5 per cent of land in future to be used for roads one would assume that London intends to exercise those other amenity options by resisting public accommodation of higher demand levels for private auto use.

Strongly reinforcing this policy of cautious road provision is the strin-

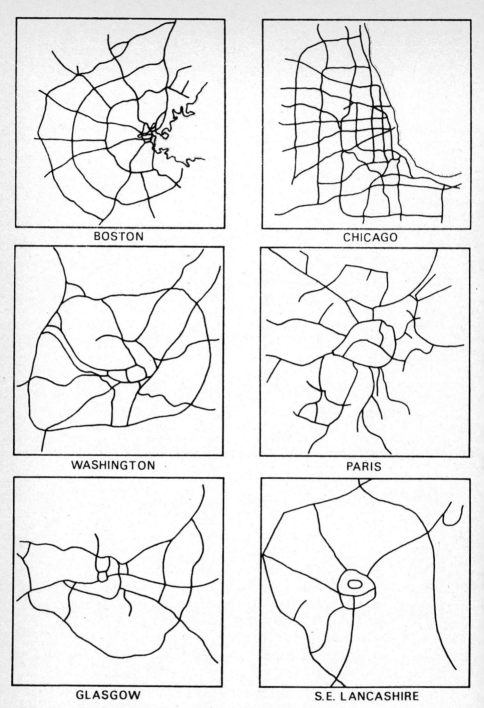

BOSTON

CHICAGO

WASHINGTON

PARIS

GLASGOW

S.E. LANCASHIRE

Fig. 7.2   Primary road networks in selected large cities.

Source: Ibid., p. 93.

Table 7.1

Primary road mileage per thousand population in London
and selected English cities, 1968

Area	Miles of principal and trunk roads per thousand population
London	0·13
West Midlands	0·14
Merseyside	0·12
SELNEC	0·17
Tyneside	0·14
West Yorkshire	0·24

Note: SELNEC refers to South-East Lancashire and North-East Cheshire.

Source: Ibid., pp. 168 and 169.

Table 7.2

Primary road mileage per million population proposed
in selected cities

Area	Proposed miles of primary road per million population
London	39
Clydeside	76+
Merseyside	55–60
SELNEC	45–50
Paris	40
Toronto	68
Boston	143
Los Angeles	147

Note: SELNEC refers to South-East Lancashire and North-East Cheshire.

Source: Ibid., pp. 168 and 169.

Table 7.3

Percentage of land used for roads in selected major cities

City	Current population (millions)	Percentage of land currently used as roads
London	7·7	11 (12½ proposed)
Liverpool	0·7	11
Paris	6·5	13
New York	7·8	35
Los Angeles	6·5	22
Boston	2·4	17
Moscow	5·0	12

Source: Ibid., p. 169.

gent restriction and control of car parking within the bounds of the Inner London Parking Area (ILPA). Between 1966 and 1971 in Central London the number of parking spaces of all types declined, the numbers of parkers at peak periods declined, and the rate of capacity use rose during peak periods, as presented by the figures in Table 7.4. We can see as well that these changes were accompanied by nearly complete elimination of on-street free parking and rises in proportionate shares of spaces falling under various controlled and private off-street categories.

Again, as we project to the future (see Table 7.5), we discover complete elimination of all uncontrolled on-street space and rather sharp control on increases in private off-street space by 1981 both for Central London and its surrounding precincts. In fact, while a fairly modest rise of about 50,000 spaces is envisioned for the Central area, virtually no change in parking space will occur in the surrounding area during the 1970s. Alternatively, projecting spatially across the entire Greater London Council (GLC) area, we find (see Table 7.6) new standards establishing parking space to floor-space ratios for offices and retail enterprises that severely limit potential automobile accommodation associated with any future increases or redistributions in such activities. The increases in ratios between old and new standards range up to six times as high for inner areas and four times as high in outer areas of Greater London.

At this point, it is difficult to say how such auto accessibility control is contributing to the living amenity in London. One can perhaps say that some deleterious effects such as rising congestion levels do not appear to

Table 7.4

Changes in parking supply and demand, London 1966–71

Type of parking	Number of spaces	Peak number of parkers	Peak occupancy	Percentage of total spaces	Percentage of total peak occupancy
1966					
On-street: free	30,000	26,208	87·4	24·0	27·6
On-street: metered	14,500	12,172	84·3	11·5	12·7
Off-street: public	25,500	17,061	67·3	20·5	17·9
Off-street: private	55,000	39,917	72·6	44·0	41·8
Total	125,000	95,358	76·4	100·0	100·0
1971					
On-street: free	2,000	1,900	95	1·9	2
On-street: metered	21,000	18,700	89	20·0	21
Off-street: public	29,000	22,000	76	27·6	25
Off-street: private	53,000	46,500	86	50·5	52
Total	105,000	89,100	85	100·0	100

Source: Tony May, 'Parking control for restraint in Greater London' *GLC Intelligence Unit Quarterly Bulletin* no. 19, June 1972, p. 35.

Table 7.5

Changes in parking space supply in the ILPA, 1970–81

Type of parking space	Central area		Remainder of ILPA	
	1970	1981	1970	1981
On-street: free	2,000	–	250,000	–
On-street: metered	21,000	31,500	12,000	152,000
On-street: residents	7,000		26,000	
Off-street: public	29,000	50,000	10,000	30,000
Off-street: private residential	17,000	26,500	78,000	160,000
Off-street: private non-residential	53,000	63,000	63,000	102,000
Total	119,000	171,000	439,000	444,000

Source: Ibid., p. 34.

Table 7.6

Parking standards for offices and shops in Greater London

Area	Spaces per square foot of gross floor area	
	Old standard*	New (GLDP) standard†
Offices		
Central area	1/2,000	1/5,000–1/12,000
Inner London	1/2,000	1/2,000–1/8,000
Outer London	1/500	1/400–1/2,000
Shops		
Central area	1/2,500	1/5,000–1/12,000
Inner London	1/2,500	1/2,000–1/8,000
Outer London	1/1,000	1/400–1/2,000

* Minimum standards.
† Maximum standards.

Source: Ibid., p. 32.

Fig. 7.3   Peak and off-peak journey speeds and parking control in Central London.

Source: GLC Intelligence ... no. 19, June 1972, p. 35.

be the result of these efforts. In fact, the concurrent rises in peak and off-peak average travel speeds and the degree of parking control in Central London (see Fig. 7.3) imply some amelioration of congestion conditions. In like manner, the comparison of amounts of road mileage added with changes in average auto speeds in different parts of Greater London between 1962 and 1970 indicate a mildly beneficial congestion reduction effect, as indicated in Table 7.7. At worst, there is no indication of rising congestion in the face of amounts of road construction of all types in all parts of the area that at best can be called nominal. On primary roads there has been a gain of about three miles per hour in speed, and for all areas and road types there has been virtually no change in speed while overall road mileage has been held roughly constant.

Infrastructural control and withholding of significantly higher levels of accommodation of auto traffic in London has been complemented by a somewhat heavier than average reliance on public transport. In comparing local public transport service levels, we find 56 public vehicle (bus and rail) miles per capita per year for London but only 29 for Rome and 26 for Paris.[2] Again, no conclusion of global dimension about benefits and costs for the agglomeration can be drawn on the basis of experience and information in hand to date. But we can note a likely degree of effective-

Table 7.7

Changes in road mileage and travel speed in
Greater London, 1962–70

GLC area and road type	Miles of road		Average speed (miles per hour)	
	1962	1970	1962	1970
GLC primary roads	81	101	28·8	32·1
Other roads				
Central area	87	102	12·4	12·1
Inner area	307	305	16·4	17·4
Central and inner areas	394	407	15·0	15·3
Outer area	938	970	24·4	24·6
All areas	1,342	1,377	19·9	20·2
All roads	1,423	1,478	20·6	21·3

Source: GLC Intelligence ... no. 16, September 1971, p. 13.

ness in holding down accessibility levels and growth pressures and attention to other elements of transport balance and, implicitly, activity compositional balance in the London agglomeration.

The difficulty of evaluating infrastructural provision over a period of time in terms of a consistent national urban policy was emphasised by our earlier quote from the GLDP demonstrating continued covergence of the national highway system on London while policies of auto accessibility containment were being followed within the urban area itself. A policy tension has thereby emerged from the local resistance to completion of the extensive circumnavigational road system that would be a logical follow-on in London to the motorway routes terminating on all sides of the area.

Infrastructural allocations in France

An attempt has been made by Prud'homme to assess for France the effectiveness of allocation of infrastructure to different areas in furtherance of national regional and urban growth objectives. A similar kind of dichotomy and policy tension to that experienced in Great Britain emerges from the implementation patterns in France.

Initially, Prud'homme hypothesises that infrastructure provision for an area by central government is a function of the population level, population growth, and political influence (measured by the proportionate share of Assembly representatives belonging to the political parties in office for the area) of the area in question. His statistical test of his proposition, however, '... suggests that central goverment subsidies to a region are a function of the population of the region (which is obvious), but not of the increase in the population of the region (which is surprising), nor of the political influence of the region. In other words, differences in per capita subsidies must be attributed to regional policy differences'.[3] The pattern of actual infrastructure and related regional assistance by central government depicted in Figure 7.4 yields a distribution of favoured and disfavoured areas largely out of accord with nominal policy objectives in France. The $T'r$ notation signifies the difference between the national average per capita expenditure by central government and the level of per capita expenditure occurring in each of the respective planning regions of France as shown in Figure 7.4.

The results of implementation then are, as Prud'homme notes, '... alien to what is supposed to be. The goal of favouring the western regions has clearly not been implemented. The central government fared a little better

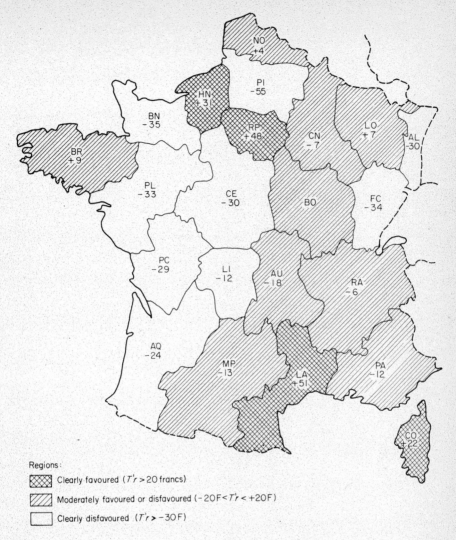

Regions:

▨ Clearly favoured ($T'r > 20$ francs)

▨ Moderately favoured or disfavoured ($-20F < T'r < +20F$)

☐ Clearly disfavoured ($T'r > -30F$)

Fig. 7.4 The pattern of central government infrastructure and related assistance in France, 1966–70.

Source: Rémy Prud'homme, 'Regional Economic Policy in France, 1962–1972, mimeo, BETURE, Paris, March 1973, p. 32.

with respect to its objectives about Nord and Lorraine: both regions received per head more than the average. But it is a surprise to see that two of the most favoured regions were the Paris region and Haute-Normandie, which are the richest regions not supposed to receive any assistance'.[4] One can infer little directly from these regional data about the urban strategies

157

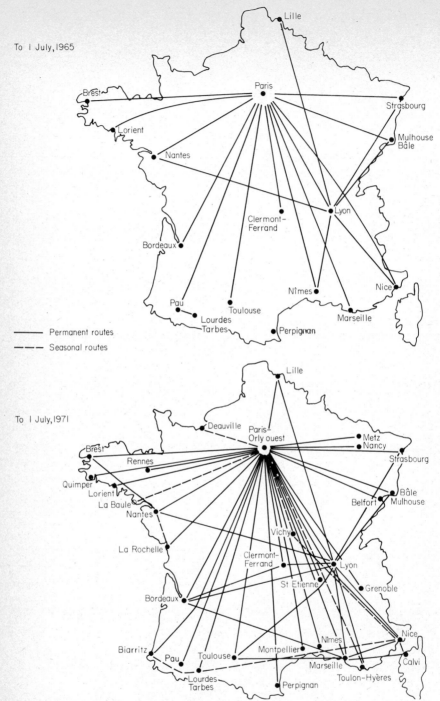

Fig. 7.5   Routes operated by Air-Inter in France, 1965—71.

Source: DATAR, *La Politique d'aménagement du territoire,* Loi de finances pour 1973, Paris, p. 83.

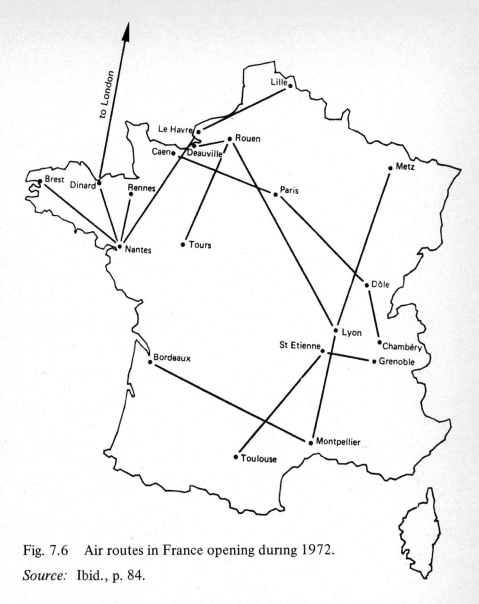

Fig. 7.6 Air routes in France opening during 1972.

Source: Ibid., p. 84.

as manifested by the *métropoles d'équilibre*, but it cannot pass without notice that most of the latter are located in regions that are not favoured by the observed pattern of infrastructural assistance.

An even closer look must be taken at French policy, and any other nations' policies, however, to assess the degree of response to need for more effective urban strategies. We are still sufficiently on the frontiers of such policy shifts and innovation not to be able to discern significant consolidations of instrument use directed at urban growth objectives

Table 7.8

Proportionate contribution of direct stimulating and indirect infrastructural measures to total employment growth in the north of the Netherlands, 1960–67

Region	Absolute increase in employment in industrial and service sectors	Total employment in 1960	Percentage increase of employment due to stimulating measures, 1960–67	Total absolute increase of employment due to stimulating measures, 1960–67	Total proportional contribution of stimulating measures
	(1)	(2)	(3)	(4) (2)×(3)/100	(5) [(4)/(1)]×100
Groningen agglomeration	10,309	66,996	7·60	5,094	49·4
Appingedam, Delfzijl	2,542	9,449	10·13	957	37·7
Groninger-Hoogland and North Westerkwartier	1,226	21,756	2·53	550	44·9
Groninger Oldambt	2,247	20,148	2·53	510	22·7
Groninger Veenkoloniën	6,178	42,982	5·06	2,175	35·2
Groninger Centrale Weidestreek	820	10,947	2·53	277	33·8
Leeuwarden	2,582	33,403	5·06	1,690	65·5
Friese Bouwstreek	2,235	31,152	2·53	788	35·3
Fries Weidegebied	3,744	41,077	5·06	2,078	55·5
Noord-Fries Zandgebied	3,746	25,860	5·06	1,309	34·9
Zuid-Fries Zandgebied	3,871	27,730	5·06	1,403	37·1
Noorddrents Randgebied	747	4,900	5·06	248	33·2
Emmen	4,638	34,905	5·06	1,766	38·1
Drentse Veenkoloniën	1,349	14,321	2·53	362	26·9
Noord-Drentse Zandgronden	2,940	25,777	5·06	1,304	44·4
Zuid-Drentse Zandgronden	2,255	14,987	5·06	758	33·6
Z.W. Drenthe	1,231	14,393	2·53	364	29·6
Kampen-Zwolle	5,460	56,240	5·06	2,846	52·1
Hardenberg	1,254	20,602	2·53	521	41·6

Source: Ad. J. Hendriks and S. Panitchpakdi, 'Regional policy in the Netherlands', mimeo, Netherlands Economic Institute, Erasmus University, Rotterdam, March 1973, p. 34.

nationally. We can see from the air routes connecting French cities that were opened by Air-Inter, the French domestic airline, mapped in Figure 7.5, that between 1965 and 1971 the dominance of Paris was clearly maintained but that efforts were made to increase the number of independent links between provincial cities. At the margin of policy reorientation, we see in

Figure 7.6 that, of 17 new air routes opening in 1972, only two connected with Paris while the remainder provided inter-provincial city services. The convergencies of four new lines each on, respectively, Nantes and Lyon — St Etienne imply new outlying foci of communication in France.

Infrastructural reinforcement for urban expansion in the Netherlands

In the Netherlands, the earlier described focus of growth promotion in the North on such sizeable centres as Groningen is estimated to have had noticeable effect. Significant shares of job growth are attributed to infrastructural and direct instrument use in the urban centres and other areas of the North, as documented in Table 7.8. Of the total job growth of about 10,300 jobs in the largest agglomeration, that of Groningen, between 1960 and 1967, nearly half, or about 5,100 were statistically attributable to governmental stimulation measures. Impressive proportionate shares of job growth in other areas of the North were estimated also to be linked with governmental assistance. These efforts have been aimed largely at traditional manufacturing job creation but with a growing awareness of the need for broader action to create and maintain balanced growth in larger industrial centres like Groningen. This latter awareness is reflected in part by recent government proposals to relocate government offices out of The Hague and the Randstad as an exemplary move for private tertiary and quaternary-sector activities.

Perhaps the best that we can say at the moment about such trends in national policy implementation is that it is not yet possible to give a verdict on their true significance. Rather, innovations under the newer urban strategies should be observed closely over the next few years.

Notes

[1] Greater London Council, *Greater London Development Plan: Public Inquiry Proof*, E.12/1, 'Transport', London, November 1970, p. 94.
[2] Ibid., p. 173.
[3] Prud'homme, op.cit., p. 29.
[4] Ibid., p. 31.

8 Government and Private Office Location Guidance

One of the most innovative lines of advance in direct policy implementation is the recently emerging combination of relocation of national level government jobs and offices out of capital cities coupled with disincentives/incentives applied in tandem to guide private sector tertiary and quaternary jobs and offices out of congested urban areas and into other promising but feasible centres of growth. Even when the government office relocations themselves do not constitute a significant proportionate share of the total activities involved, the implication is that such government action displays commitment and sets an example for private enterprise. But, in addition, the analysis and understanding provided by out-movement and new location patterns of large bureaucratic enterprises in the public sector sets in motion a crucial learning process that informs policy for future action in both public and private sectors. Certainly, the very act of trying to redistribute into alternative urban areas the service and management jobs involved, addresses one of the core issues that we raised earlier concerning the necessary and sufficient conditions for bal-' anced urban growth to be generated and maintained. Against this background we can assess some of the more vigorous and forceful attempts at such direct instrument application.

Relocating government offices from London

An extended review and recommendation for central government headquarters job dispersal from London has just culminated in publication (in June 1973) of the so-called 'Hardman Report' in Great Britain.[1] The principal objects of the dispersal policy are the headquarters offices in London, i.e. those within 16 miles of Charing Cross. Some other non-governmental bodies financed by government are included but public corporations do not fall under the dispersal policy. The universe of central government jobs in the United Kingdom, totalling some half million, and their functional and geographical distribution appear as in Table 8.1. Nearly 70 per cent of these jobs are already in regional and local offices around

Table 8.1

Geographical and functional distribution of central government staff in the United Kingdom

Area	Headquarters staff		Regional and local staff		All staff	
	No.	Percentage of total staff	No.	Percentage of total staff	No.	Percentage of total staff
London (Inner and Outer)	95,886	19·2	47,824	9·6	143,710	28·8
Rest of South East Region	11,562	2·3	70,128	14·0	81,690	16·3
Rest of the UK	45,335	9·0	221,031	44·2	266,366	53·2
Locations outside the UK	977	0·2	7,435	1·5	8,412	1·7
Totals	153,760	30·7	346,418	69·3	500,178	100·0

Source: The Prime Minister and Minister for the Civil Service, *The Dispersal of Government Work from London,* HMSO, London, June 1973, p. 20.

the country, but only 11 per cent of such total staff represents headquarters functions, which are those addressing national or non-regional/non-local concerns. At present about 62 per cent of headquarters jobs are in Greater London, about 95,500 jobs, which form the pool from which dispersal can occur.

The actual number of London headquarters jobs under active review by Hardman for possible dispersal amounted to a smaller total, namely 86,133 after elimination of those jobs thought to be tied to London irrevocably by nature of their function. These latter constituted the higher or highest level decision-making functions across all departments and independent agencies. The dual analytical approach of the Hardman team was to evaluate, respectively: (1) the operating functions and needs of the departments in terms of 'blocks of work' carried out by them and the damage or benefit arising from denial of a London location; and (2) the potential of a wide array of cities and urban areas to serve as locations for these blocks of work and their constituent jobs including serving the needs of the types of people filling the latter and their families.

Before presenting and assessing the dispersal conclusions and recommendations of the Hardman review, it should be noted that it is not a *de novo* exercise but builds on a sizeable base of existing experience in the United Kingdom. After an earlier review of a similar nature, by Sir Gilbert Flemming in May 1963, the government acted to disperse about 50,000 jobs. Roughly 32,000 have been relocated and 18,000 are scheduled for relocation as at the time of writing, with the geographic distribution shown by the percentages in Table 8.2. For the moves completed between 1963 and 1972, cities in some of the Assisted Areas fared rather well, with Scotland receiving 20 per cent and the North and North West region cities together receiving approximately another 30 per cent. Of course, the wealthy and congested South East also received nearly 30 per cent of the offices in this first round, but suffered a notable drop to 10 per cent of the scheduled moves yet to come. Most of the Assisted Areas maintain their good shares of the scheduled moves after 1972 with Wales being an enormous gainer, its share rising from about 9 to 43 per cent of the total.

The attractiveness of retaining offices in the South East is fairly clear from the pattern in these earlier office dispersals, but there is also evident

Table 8.2

Central government office jobs relocated or scheduled for relocation from London by 1972

Regional location of cities receiving office jobs	Jobs relocated, May 1963 – October 1972		Jobs scheduled for relocation at October 1972	
	No. of posts placed outside London	Percentage of overall total placed outside London	No. of posts to be placed outside London	Percentage of overall total to be placed outside London
Scotland	6,481	20·2	4,476	24·6
North	3,377	10·5	790	4·3
North West	5,997	18·7	1,918	10·5
Yorkshire and Humberside	783	2·4	55	0·3
Wales	2,826	8·8	7,784	42·7
East Midlands	746	2·3	140	0·8
West Midlands	279	0·9	0	
East Anglia	1,192	3·7	0	
South West	1,332	4·2	1,185	6·5
South East	9,004	28·1	1,861	10·2
Total	32,017	100·0	18,209	100·0

Source: Ibid., pp. 28–30.

an effort to shift activity northward and westward (Wales). As noted, the Hardman review attempts to balance off against any losses in operating efficiency and mission fulfilment capability of the governmental departments. From the side of assessing the potential of various cities to absorb given levels and compositions of government employment, we find in the Hardman Report conclusions of a self-limiting nature with respect to creating self-generating capabilities to shift into tertiary—quaternary jobs in lagging urban areas. The nature of the approach is expressed best in the words of the report itself:

> The capacity of locations was considered in the light of certain points, including the Government's wish to disperse work to a few major locations, rather than scattering small units over many places. In the case of locations other than most of those which are associated with a particular Department (see paragraph 16), it has accordingly been considered whether they could sustain a dispersal amounting to a few thousand posts.
>
> The results of interdepartmental studies, now confirmed by the composition of the blocks of work recommended for dispersal, suggested that, as a working guide, half the posts dispersed from London would be in the local recruitment grades and the questions asked derive from the 'efficiency' considerations noted above in paragraph 2. Conclusions on potential capacity in respect of accommodation and staffing — leaving aside any questions of distance — are set out below.

Region	Location	Capacity*
Scotland	Glasgow	5,000
Wales	Cardiff	
	Newport	5,000
Northern	Darlington	500
	Tyneside	2,000
	Teesside	5,000
North Western	Central Lancashire New Town (Preston—Leyland—Chorley)	3,000
	Manchester	3,000
	Merseyside	3,000
	Runcorn	500
Yorkshire/Humberside	Leeds or	3,000
	Greater Bradford	2,000
East Anglia	Norwich	500

West Midlands	Coventry	1,500
South Western	Bristol	1,000 or
		2,500†
	Plymouth	5,000
	Swindon	1,000
South Eastern	Basingstoke	500
	Croydon	—
	Milton Keynes	5,000‡
	Southend	500

Notes: * This is in terms of the total number of posts which could efficiently be absorbed, that is both posts in Civil Service grades where mobility is a condition of service which will be filled mostly by staff moving from London, and posts where there is no mobility requirement and most of which will be filled by local recruitment.
† Over longer term.
‡ Could be more over longer term.

The capacity figures have been taken as one of the bases in working out proposals as to the number of posts which could be dispersed to particular locations. (The method of doing this is described in Appendix 6.) The capacity figures are in terms of the number of posts removed, whether these posts are to be filled by officers transferring with their work or by local recruitment.[2]

From the viewpoint of our earlier discussion of growth trends and policy strategies, it is a boon that the report focuses on assessing conditions within different kinds of urban areas rather than large regions and proposes concentration of relatively large numbers of jobs in selected locales. On the other hand, the neat round figure maximum of 5,000 jobs as a capacity limit appears again and again for urban areas of vastly different size and character. By the report's own definitions, Glasgow appears condemned to an ultimate absorptive capacity of 5,000 jobs while Milton Keynes, presently open space in the main and even at its target size only a small fraction of the size of Glasgow, is judged to have the same capacity in the visible future and possibly more later on.

The principle, enunciated earlier, of temporally interweaving direct instruments, which are capitalising on current growth potentials, with indirect or infrastructural/co-ordinative instruments, which are raising growth potentials through successive time periods and programmed rounds of application, appears to be applied in the case of Milton Keynes recognising its new town status. By implication, such an advantage does not seem to be imputed to Glasgow or such areas as Teesside, Cardiff/ Newport, or Plymouth. To go to the trouble, in the first place, of establishing a dispersal policy aimed at decongesting one area and inducing balanced growth in others without carefully determining the nature of attendant policies required for raising absorptive capacities over time, so that places like Glasgow could anticipate measurable inputs of public and private office jobs (say 15–20,000 over the next five to seven years) instead of indefinite ceilings at nominal levels, would seem to be a gratuitous and self-defeating exercise.

The Hardman Report probably is within proper bounds to estimate conservatively the amount of urban growth support that can be offered safely without too severely compromising government efficiency (i.e. costs) and effectiveness. The nature of the job 'trade-offs' between areas when one opts for 'efficient', 'regional', and 'compromise' (the recommended) solutions are shown by the alternative distributions of the 31,427 jobs finally recommended for dispersal, out of the original total of 86,133 jobs that were under review.

FIRST ALTERNATIVE – THE 'EFFICIENT' SOLUTION

Department	Number of posts in blocks of work to be dispersed	Suggested receiving location
Ministry of Agriculture, Fisheries and Food .	1,250	Coventry
Agricultural Research Council	140	Coventry
Civil Service Department	707	
comprising:	357	Norwich
	300	Basingstoke
	50	Sunningdale
Her Majesty's Customs and Excise	500	Southend
Ministry of Defence	10,890	Milton Keynes
Department of Employment	1,540	
comprising:	1,400	Liverpool
	140	Liverpool (with Home Office)

Department	Number	Location
Department of the Environment (DOE)	1,248	Bristol
DOE (Property Services Agency)	4,100	Cardiff
Foreign and Commonwealth Office (FCO)	986	Bristol
FCO (Overseas Development Administration)	1,177	Manchester
Department of Health and Social Security	1,480	
comprising:	500	Newcastle
	980	Central Lancashire New Town
Home Office	1,437	Liverpool
Criminal Injuries Compensation Board	83	Liverpool
Board of Inland Revenue	1,610	Leeds
Natural Environment Research Council	191	Swindon
Office of Population Censuses and Surveys	920	Titchfield
Science Research Council	388	Swindon
Her Majesty's Stationery Office	380	Norwich
Department of Trade and Industry	1,800	
comprising:	1,442	Cardiff/Newport
(Laboratory of the Government Chemist)	358	Teddington
Export Credits Guarantee Department	600	Cardiff
Total	31,427	

SECOND ALTERNATIVE – THE 'REGIONAL' SOLUTION

Department	Number of posts in blocks of work to be dispersed	Suggested receiving location
Ministry of Agriculture, Fisheries and Food	1,250	Liverpool

Agricultural Research Council	140	Liverpool
Civil Service Department	707	
comprising:	357	Norwich
	300	Basingstoke
	50	Sunningdale
Her Majesty's Customs and Excise	500	Southend
Ministry of Defence	10,890	
comprising:	6,218	Cardiff
	4,672	Milton Keynes
Department of Employment	1,540	
comprising:	1,400	Liverpool
	140	Plymouth (with Home Office)
Department of the Environment (DOE)	1,248	Bristol
DOE (Property Services Agency)	4,100	Teesside
Foreign and Commonwealth Office (FCO)	986	Liverpool
FCO (Overseas Development Administration)	1,177	Glasgow
Department of Health and Social Security	1,480	
comprising:	500	Newcastle
	980	Central Lancashire New Town
Home Office	1,437	Plymouth
Criminal Injuries Compensation Board	83	Plymouth
Board of Inland Revenue	1,610	Plymouth
Natural Environment Research Council	191	Swindon
Office of Population Censuses and Surveys	920	Central Lancashire New Town
Science Research Council	388	Swindon
Her Majesty's Stationery Office	380	Norwich

Department of Trade and Industry	1,800	
comprising:	1,142	Newcastle
	300	Newport
(Laboratory of the Government Chemist)	358	Teddington
Export Credits Guarantee Department	600	Glasgow

Total	31,427	

Department	Number of posts in blocks of work to be dispersed	Suggested receiving location
Ministry of Agriculture, Fisheries and Food	1,250	Manchester
Agricultural Research Council	140	Manchester
Civil Service Department	707	
comprising:	357	Norwich
	300	Basingstoke
	50	Sunningdale
Her Majesty's Customs and Excise	500	Southend
Ministry of Defence	10,890	Milton Keynes
Department of Employment	1,540	
comprising:	1,400	Liverpool
	140	Plymouth (with Home Office)
Department of the Environment (DOE)	1,248	Bristol
DOE (Property Services Agency)	4,100	Cardiff
Foreign and Commonwealth Office (FCO)	986	Central Lancashire New Town (Preston–Leyland–Chorley)

FCO (Overseas Development Administration)	1,177	Glasgow
Department of Health and Social Security	1,480	
comprising:	500	Newcastle
	980	Central Lancashire New Town
Home Office	1,437	Plymouth
Criminal Injuries Compensation Board	83	Plymouth
Board of Inland Revenue	1,610	Teesside
Natural Environment Research Council	191	Swindon
Office of Population Censuses and Surveys	920	Central Lancashire New Town
Science Research Council	388	Swindon
Her Majesty's Stationery Office	380	Norwich
Department of Trade and Industry	1,800	
comprising:	1,442	Cardiff/Newport
(Laboratory of the Government Chemist)	358	Teddington
Export Credits Guarantee Department	600	Liverpool
Total	31,427[3]	

One could begin by questioning the criteria and analyses that went into distributing jobs under the efficient and regional solutions, and these will undoubtedly be debated hotly and vigorously as decisions are taken for the relocations over the coming few years. Unfortunately, neither time nor space permit such inquiry here. But we can see that even the 'regional solution' falls far below the report's estimates of absorptive capacities in key areas such as Glasgow and the Central Lancashire New Town. Further, the 'recommended solution' appears to favour the 'efficient solution' job distribution more than the 'regional', as Milton Keynes captures nearly 11,000 defence jobs (over twice its estimated immediate potential) while Glasgow and Teesside limp along with about 1,200 and 1,600 jobs, respectively.

Finally, we should mention that not just the number of the jobs shifted outward is important, but also the quality, e.g. routine tertiary versus judgemental quaternary work. The intention of moving out of London higher decision-making positions is well served by the report's approach of evaluating blocks of work with full hierarchies of job types and responsibilities within them. This helps to resist the tendency systematically to sift out the more routine level functions in each department to be sloughed off to the 'regions'. This latter orientation cannot be too heavily resisted, since about 55,000 jobs under the review, containing many higher grade positions, are remaining in London for 'efficiency' reasons, not to mention the thousands of other jobs that were excluded initially from the review because of their *prima facie* close ties to central decision-making in London.

In spite of any problems recounted here, the government dispersal attempt is a significant contribution to the combined public and private-sector activity moves from London to other readjusting or growing urban localities. It could add impetus to the very recent shifts to higher levels and rates of Office Development Permit (ODP) issues in the Outer Metropolitan Area (OMA) and Outer South East (OSE) over those for the City of London and Central London, as depicted in Figure 8.1. Central London has maintained a higher level and, on average, about as fast a pace of permit issues as have either of the outer areas beyond Greater London in the South East. The downturns in permit issues since 1971 in the central areas and OMA have been in contrast to a sharp upturn in the OSE. More vigorous pursuit of government office dispersal may reinforce government ability and determination to guide further amounts of private sector office locations out of Greater London through firmer ODP restraint in the inner areas. The critical deficiency in this system at present is the lack of any significant subsidisation of office location in urban areas outside of Greater London. As with the recently launched French scheme for subsidies to tertiary sector enterprises locating outside of the Paris region, direct incentives need to be added to the instrument set in Great Britain for potentially effective guidance of office locations in desired directions.

Government office relocations from Stockholm

A review of government operations and potential receiving urban locales, roughly parallel to that just described for the United Kingdom, has been carried out in Sweden with the aim of relocating about 11,000 central government jobs from Stockholm to selected urban areas between 1975

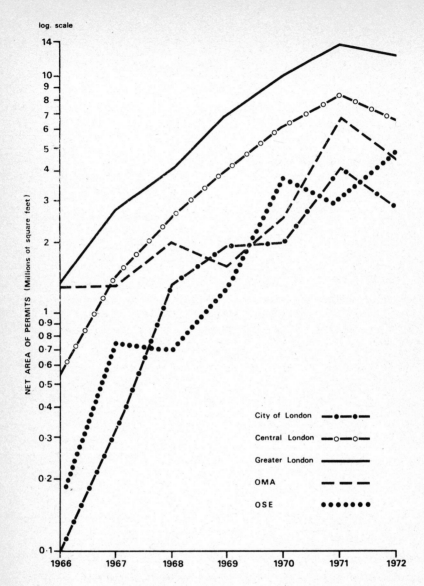

Fig. 8.1 Office development permits in South East England, 1966–72.

Note: At its inception the office development control applied to all projects of 3.000 sq. ft or more. The exemption limit was raised to 10,000 sq. ft in the OSE in July 1967, in the OMA in February 1969 and in Greater London in December 1970.

Source: Department of the Environment, *Strategic Planning ...,* op. cit., p. 56a.

174

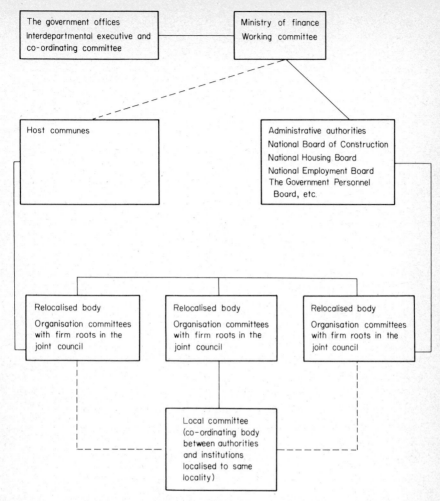

Fig. 8.2 Central government organisation for the execution of relocalisation of government departments in Sweden.

Source: Working Party on New Patterns of Settlement, *Swedish Government Relocation Policy in Norrköping,* European Free Trade Association, Geneva 1973, p. 16.

and 1980. The prime mover in initiating the review and setting in motion the process of governmental office relocation was the Minister of Finance who called for a new commission to make a study and recommendations for helping to relieve pressure on the Stockholm area and simultaneously create tertiary–quaternary type jobs in the larger urban centres designated for growth.

The central government organisation for carrying out the office relocations is depicted in Figure 8.2. At the central level, the Ministry of Finance working committee assures an across-the-board assessment of all functions in the independent government boards subject to possible relocation. Through local planning in the selected host urban areas, a well-thought-out settling-in procedure is established for jobs and people going to any particular locality. The extent of central/local co-operative planning is detailed in Figure 8.3, wherein the pilot executive plan for office relocations to Norrköping shows the degree and nature of local response required for new growth of the anticipated character. [4]

What kinds of jobs and offices are to move? As in the British case, the ministries making key decisions and requiring close liaison with the Riksdag or Parliament were excluded from consideration. Likewise, any of the independent boards — basic line agencies implementing government programmes — with high policy content were removed from the list of potential movers. This would include boards such as the National Labour Market Board, National Board of Health and Welfare, and the National Education and Policy Boards. Frequency of contact with ministries and parliament was a major device for ranking boards in terms of those that would suffer least from a move out of Stockholm.

In the less politically sensitive boards remaining there was an attempt, nonetheless, to move integral 'blocks of work' with the full hierarchy of decision-making and support personnel as in the British case. In virtually all instances, this amounts to selecting entire boards or research institutes for moves as integral units. Further, there was an explicit effort to group boards on a functional basis in the respective new locations, e.g. groupings of research institutes, testing facilities, and regulatory functions for a particular private sector such as forestry, housing, and so on.

There was an explicit intention to affect favourably the occupational structures of the 15 finally selected receiving areas by introducing these service, technical, and management jobs into the local labour markets. For this reason, the number of receiving locations was kept low and only primary centres, the next size class below the three metropolitan areas, were selected to ensure a minimal degree of growth potential. In the recent past, between 1966 and 1970 (see Table 8.3), the levels and rates of growth in numbers of central government employees has been noticeably above the national average in the three metropolitan areas, slightly above average in the other major towns (roughly, the primary centres), and below average in the smaller centres in the lagging North and South-central parts of Sweden. The government office relocations are aimed at further promoting balanced growth in this major town category below the

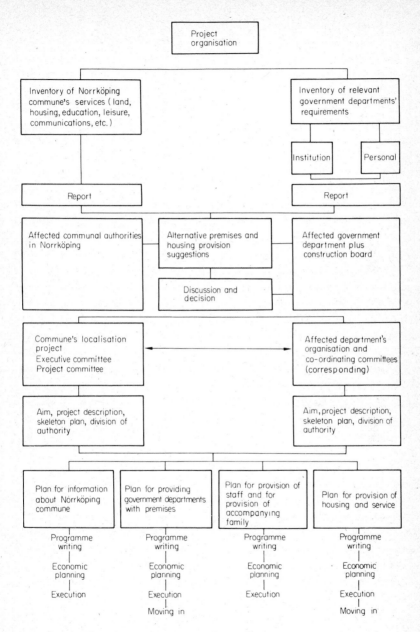

Fig. 8.3 Executive plan for relocalisation from Stockholm of various government departments to Norrköping.

Source: Ibid, p. 19.

Table 8.3

Changes in the number of central government employees in different
urban areas of Sweden between 1966 and 1970

| Urban area (group of municipal blocks) | No. of government employees | | Percentage change |
	1966	1970	1966–1970
Stockholm	93,000	107,000	+ 15·6
Göteborg and Malmö	44,000	51,000	+ 17·8
Major towns	93,000	106,000	+ 13·4
South-central Sweden	50,000	55,000	+ 11·5
Northern dense areas	31,000	34,000	+ 9·9
Northern sparse areas	15,000	16,000	+ 6·3
Total	326,000	369,000	+ 12·7

Note: Urban areas (municipal blocks) are classified according to their local and regional populations. *Major towns* have more than 90,000 inhabitants within 30 km. of the centre and more than 300,000 within 100 km. The municipalities in *South-central Sweden* have the same regional basis but less than 90,000 inhabitants on a local score. Those in *Northern dense areas* have between 27,000 and 90,000 inhabitants and less than 300,000 regional, while municipalities in *Northern sparse areas* (mostly the inland districts) have less than 27,000 local and less than 300,000 regional inhabitants.

Source: Swedish Ministry of Labour and Housing, op. cit., p. 17.

metropolitan level. Seven of the cities selected are in the North, four are depressed localities with socio-economic structural problems, and four were selected on the basis of unique infrastructural advantages, e.g. university facilities.

These selections reflect the current assistance priorities of the Parliament, which are, roughly, the North, the South-east, and a prohibition of assistance for the three metropolitan areas. In fact, virtually none of the relocated offices will go to either Malmö or Göteborg. The difficulty in making such precise and concentrated location allocations is reflected in the fact that practically every local authority in Sweden approached the relocation commission about the possibility of being considered as candidates for receiving a board or other government agency or facility. This was so even though only primary centres could be candidates according to the publicly established criteria of the commission. Political and administrative influence operate incessantly to diffuse the geographic distribution of growth assistance. On the opposite side, there was also hostile reaction from the community in Stockholm emanating from the fear that such job dispersal would generate measurable negative multiplier effects on income in the urban area.

So far, the government is sticking by its planned locations, but is taking a pragmatic trial-and-error approach to implementation. The latter is reflected in the fact that, while it is recognised that various infrastructural reinforcements to growth could raise the effectiveness of the effort, there are no current government commitments to tie any other investments to the office relocations. Existing infrastructural advantages are being capitalised on with something of a wait-and-see attitude; for instance, there are a couple of specialised graduate schools in Norrköping that could offer support to some of the new government activities and people but no plans exist to consolidate and expand these into a larger university facility. In addition, it is foreseen that slightly higher levels and perhaps altered patterns of travel might occur which could necessitate airline route and scheduling changes. But nothing of a leading nature is contemplated in that infrastructural area, only close watching for possible future demand changes generated by the direct instrument actions and related rises in private activity.

Government voluntary consultations with private enterprise in Sweden

These government office relocations in Sweden are accompanied by a relatively weak and ineffective system of private industry 'location consultations'. All private manufacturing and service (retail, banking, insurance, real estate and other) enterprises are required by law to consult with the National Labour Market Board (NLMB) for any new or changed location involving 500 or more square metres of floor space if the enterprise is at present located, or wishes to locate, in any one of the three metropolitan areas of Stockholm, Göteborg, or Malmö. Even though the consultations are required to take place before building permits can be issued, the advice given by government need be taken only on a voluntary basis by the private firm concerned in each case. This system became institutionalised in April 1971 and replaces an earlier more informal procedure of *ad hoc* negotiations between government and selected very large or important enterprises embarking on location decisions.

179

The volume of consultations has not been impressive to date — about 300 between April 1971 and May 1973, due in large part, officials estimate, to recent recessionary difficulties in the national economy. It is felt, by the implementers of the policy, that the threshold of 500 square metres of space utilised means that virtually all manufacturing enterprise locations are included but that a measurable percentage of service establishments may be excluded although figures are not available on the latter.[5] A further difficulty with service firms using office space accrues from the fact that about 40 per cent of such space involved in the consultations is controlled by speculative real estate developers with whom the actual NLMB negotiations are conducted. So the ultimate occupants of the subject premises are not consulted and their identity remains unknown to the government policy implementers. In France this problem is addressed in direct fashion by the double permit system, wherein a construction authorisation is issued for the so-called *bureau en blanc* to speculative developers and then a subsequent occupancy permit is issued to the tenant or purchaser of such space at time of occupancy. In the latter case, control is extended to the rate and mix of the employing enterprises themselves.

The results of these consultations to date have been virtually nil — from 300 firms only five accepted government advice and moved from the metropolitan areas; two to the general aid area in the North, and three to the South-east and South-central parts of the country. Altogether, 100 jobs were involved. In face of this lack of result, regulations in the existing system have been tightened and investigation is under way to assess desirability of a true control system. Beginning in July 1973, firms must provide formal analyses with facts and data supporting the reasons why they must remain in the metropolitan areas. Even here, though, the NLMB will be relying on data supplied by private firms and will not conduct their own independent analyses because of insufficient staff resources. Further, there is a commission studying the possibility of instituting a full-scale permit control or penalty tax, or other variant type of system as exists in France and the United Kingdom and as proposed in the Netherlands. It is expected that several years will elapse before any possible legislation materialises.

The administrative machinery certainly exists in Sweden for implementing an office and industry guidance system if it were desired to authorise and activate one. The NLMB is comprised of a network of county boards which at present require private firms to provide three-to-five-year expansion plans so that new locations nationally can be anticipated. Even though there is no direct control system operating, there is emerging a related group of indirect and narrowly defined disincentive tools. Functionally related infrastructure to support business locations is heavily subsidised in the North, but in the metropolitan areas firms are charged the full cost of such provision. Under recent environmental quality legislation, the National Franchise Board determines the amount of pollution allowable from any new major 'polluting industry' location. The Board establishes the rules which are then applied against a firm *after* location permission has been granted. Costs assessed against a firm could be high enough to cause eventual withdrawal from some intentions to locate in particular areas. In certain circumstances, no initial location permission will be granted for selected highly sensitive environmental locations.

Experimenting with government office relocation from Bonn

The Federal Republic of Germany presently has no governmental or private sector office location guidance system functioning, but the occasion of establishing a new agency for protection of the environment has given rise to a ministerial request for evaluating alternative locations for these new Federal jobs and their office facilities. The Federal Minister for Regional Planning, Public Works, and Urban Planning,

> ...commissioned the Federal Research Institute for Land Use and Regional Planning on 19 January 1973 to produce a short expert opinion on the question of a suitable location for the Federal Office for the Protection of the Environment. Fifteen different places were surveyed in all.... Regional Planning goals and goals for an effective Federal Office for the Protection of the Environment were to be brought into the evaluation. A total of 37 criteria were derived from these two objective categories and with these a comparable, verifiable assessment of the individual locations was made.[6]

While no firm figures were available at the time of the assessment, it was estimated that about 500 jobs ranging from tertiary through quaternary type functions would be generated in the chosen locale. The mission of the new office includes: creation of an environmental planning information system; central documentation; policy guidance services to determine allocation of functional Federal department responsibilities and resources to furthering environmental protection and research; providing a secretariat for working groups and conferences in the field; and to provide other staff, publicity, and non-ministerial tasks in the field. A full hierarchy of decision-making through high grade technical positions addressing national concerns would be tied to the ultimate location.

As with the previously recounted British and Swedish exercises, specific balancing-off between functional operating effectiveness and efficiency and regional and urban growth objectives occurs in this West German exercise of government office location assessment. The Federal report points out that these two fundamentally different categories of objectives turn out to be somewhat opposed to one another so that the regional objective of creating equivalent living conditions in different areas must be furthered without seriously compromising the functioning capacity of the Federal office work.

The specific criteria of evaluation in the area of 'functioning capacity' consist of: (1) maintenance of a favourable system of contacts with other organisations, e.g. other Federal agencies, Land (state) parliaments, local authorities, educational/research organisations, local authorities, pri-

Table 8.4

Alternative rankings of West German cities as candidates for Federal office location

Rank	Ratio of 'regional' criteria to 'functioning' criteria weighting			
	70/30 weighting	50/50 weighting	30/70 weighting	Zero regional weighting
1	Kaiserslautern	Kaiserslautern	Mannheim	Bonn
2	Kassel	Karlsruhe	Bonn	Mannheim
3	Wilhelmshaven	Kassel	Dortmund	Wuppertal
4	Oldenburg	Dortmund	Karlsruhe	Hannover
5	Saarbrücken	Wilhelmshaven	Hannover	Dortmund
6	Karlsruhe	Mannheim	Wuppertal	Karlsruhe
7	Konstanz	Oldenburg	Kaiserslautern	Stuttgart
8	Dortmund	Saarbrücken	Kassel	Recklinghausen
9	Mannheim	Hannover	Recklinghausen	Kaiserslautern
10	Hannover	Bonn	Stuttgart	Saarbrücken
11	Recklinghausen	Konstanz	Saarbrücken	Kassel
12	Bonn	Wuppertal	Wilhelmshaven	Konstanz
13	Wuppertal	Recklinghausen	Oldenburg	Wilhelmshaven
14	Stuttgart	Stuttgart	Konstanz	Oldenburg
15	Berlin	Berlin	Berlin	Berlin

Source: Karl Ganser et al., 'The location for the planned Office for the Protection of the Environment', mimeo, Federal Research Institute for Land Use and Regional Planning, Bonn, February 1973, pp. 88–91 of an English translation.

vate interest groups, and international entities; (2) access to an adequate labour market, and access to an adequate set of private and public externalities to maintain competitive capital and operating costs for the office over its lifetime and to provide appropriate socio-cultural and recreational amenities for workers and families. From the standpoint of regional growth objectives the criteria consist of the potential for reducing unequal opportunities, as a result of the Federal office location, through generating equivalent (1) housing conditions (size, quality and price); (2) working conditions (job security, occupational choice, and promotional opportunity); (3) income conditions (levels and increases); (4) provision of goods and services from the private sector (price and range of choice); (5) provision of public infrastructure (full and efficient use of utilities and services); and (6) accessibility to environmental amenities (naturally endowed areas for leisure time; pollution, nuisance, and stress levels).

These criteria certainly are inclusive of the major policy concerns of urban growth that we discussed in the first section of this book. But the Federal report issues its own caveat on interpretation of its results, mainly because of a severe time limitation on its analysis and rush to present its conclusions for decision-making purposes. For the alternative rankings of West German cities as candidates for the Federal office, as shown below, 'The most important limitations result from present insufficient information about the size and organisation of the Federal Office for the Protection of the Environment, from poor formulation of the individual criteria, the merely provisional physical demarcation of the macro-location [the cities and surrounding areas], the insufficiently substantial weighting of the criteria, and disregard for the qualities of the micro-locations [form and structure within the cities]'.[7]

Under each of the criteria noted above, raw numerical scores were developed for each of the 15 potential locations based on available measures of attributes pertaining to each criterion. These were then weighted according to their perceived importance in the judgement of the evaluators, e.g. ease and availability of contacts received highest weighting under the objective category of 'capacity to function' of the Federal office. The rankings of the cities were then determined under subsequent alternative weightings of the scores achieved by each city under the respective 'function' and 'regional' objective categories. In Table 8.4 we can see the relative success of the various candidate areas when the weighting of regional criteria to functioning criteria is set, respectively, at ratios of 70/30, 50/50, 30/70, and zero for the regional criteria, thereby giving full and sole weight to functioning capacity.

The opposition between the two sets of objectives is reflected in the roughly obverse rankings of cities when the heavier weighted regional ranking (70/30) is compared with the heavier and completely weighted functional rankings (30/70 and zero regional). Moving from the former to the latter, cities like Kaiserslautern, Kassel, and Wilhelmshaven drop from top rankings to much lower ones while, conversely, cities like Bonn, Mannheim, and Wuppertal rise to compete for top ranking. These kinds of shifts in city rank in the office location competition are in accord with the heavy weighting given to business or functional contacts and the hypothesis put forth '... that intensity of contacts is not primarily a question of money but of time and effort. As geographical distance increases, contacts have been found to be sparser and less productive, even if there is no restriction on expense'.[8]

This suggests, as we argued before, that any direct instrument application decisions are largely captives of existing growth potential in an area *vis-à-vis* the survival needs of the 'directly productive' public or private activities. Commitment of infrastructural investment in such localities would then appear necessary to accelerate the pace of growth and permit feasible higher levels of direct assistance to job producing enterprises that could be capitalising on successively higher plateaus of required externality influence. Such co-ordination of instrument application focused on selected urban localities is absent in West Germany, as in virtually all other countries evaluated; therefore, the present pilot effort at office location guidance must work in isolation of other relevant instrument applications. Nonetheless the Federal evaluation just discussed explicitly identifies other critical dimensions of growth assistance and brings forth pressure for their future serious consideration.

Notes

[1] The Prime Minister and Minister for the Civil Service, *The Dispersal of Government Work from London*, HMSO, London, June 1973.

[2] Ibid., p. 60.

[3] Ibid., pp. 12, 14 and 15.

[4] For a more detailed assessment of conditions in Norrköping and the types of government jobs to be relocated there, see: Working Party on New Patterns of Settlement, *Swedish Government Relocation Policy in Norrköping*, European Free Trade Association, Geneva, January 1973.

[5] These and other subjective estimates concerning the operation and effect of the location consultations are based on personal interviews with staff of the National Labour Market Board by the author on 5 June 1973

in Stockholm. These meetings and necessary language translation were arranged and provided by Mr Sture Persson of the Civildepartment.

⁶ Karl Ganser, et al., 'The location for the planned Office for the Protection of the Environment', mimeo, Federal Research Institute for Land Use and Regional Planning, Bonn, February 1973, p. 1 of an English translation.

⁷ Ibid., p. 3.

⁸ Ibid., p. 37.

PART IV

Concluding Perspectives and Future Implications

9 Private Decisions and Public Policy Planning

A fundamental dilemma posed by attempts to implement strategies of urban growth distribution is reflected in the task of balancing off against one another, in mixed private/public economies and open democratic societies, the macro-social good nationally with the diverse micro-interests and well-being of individuals, groups and organisations that are rooted in and associated with present and future living conditions in varied localities. No efforts nationally aimed at redistributing urban area growth potentials — lowering some and raising others — are likely ever to be feasible politically without careful and sensitive attention to local and individual compensation for the inevitable dislocations arising from such publicly directed redistributions. Just as a set of national defence policies is required in a flexible and evolving framework that changes over time with perceptions and realities of 'national security' needs, so could a set of national urban growth policies be envisaged that would address on a continuing basis the concerns we identified in our introductory section.

In general, people make their choices on where and how to live on the basis of perceived values to be realised and negative factors to be avoided and minimised. Past patterns — even recent ones — show us only what people have perceived. It is critical for policy development to assess these decisions *at the margin*; to evaluate the structural changes that are or are not altering the trends. Careful analysis of any changes in *perceptions* that are being translated into changes in *preferences and actual locational patterns* must be linked to analysis of conditions that are associated with, and perhaps causing, such preferential shifts.

The changes in preferences, it can be realistically assumed, lag behind changes in conditions that provide information for individuals making decisions on location or life style in the private market. If policy is 'double lagged' by responding only to average decisions in the past, rather than current decisions at the margin, then it may respond too late to take action when costs are reasonable and problems can be avoided. An example of changing 'conditions' that have led to shifts in perceptions and location patterns is that of water pollution, where a double-lagged policy response may now involve inordinately large outlays to revive waterways

189

to useable status for recreational and potable water purposes, let alone to avoid future deterioration.

Just as national full employment policies provide on-going frameworks in which continually to *anticipate,* debate, and implement specific policies and actions to avoid emerging perceived problems, so would national urban growth policies provide vehicles for such activity. While a full-employment or macro-economic stabilisation policy does not dictate against the desires and preferences of the populace directly as to the kinds of jobs to be held or whether or not one works at all, it does deal with the hard policy choices between controlling inflation versus higher unemployment rates or lowering general interest rates to stimulate housing production versus overstimulating other capital investment. The whole apparatus of price and wage controls does not affect wage-earners versus wealth-holders equally, nor does it affect all wage-earners equally; but such controls are, from time to time (viz. the United States and the United Kingdom), deemed necessary for general social welfare in spite of their selective restrictiveness for many groups in the population.

Similar difficult trade-offs appear to be in the making with respect to present trends of urban growth around nations. Recently, in the United States, some Florida communities along the Atlantic shore have been raising building and land development standards, presumably to slow the rate of growth and preserve desired values that are threatened by market trends. This could well prove to be a restrictive policy that limits the choices of thousands (or millions) of potential future Florida residents who prefer that living environment. Other selective controls in Florida, such as stiff licensing requirements for physicians and other professions, act to maintain selectively various social and economic, as well as environmental, balances in the future growth of Florida. Plans in Oregon to slow growth indicate a rising awareness of and desire to make these kinds of trade-offs in certain 'threatened' localities and to avoid replication of the California growth experience.

A national perspective – and set of policies evolved over time – would be desirable to achieve more effective and equitable attainment of what may often be legitimate and laudable goals. Growth pressures are not likely to be successfully resisted at the local or even regional level when they involve powerful incentives and national flows of people and activities responding to *presently* perceived attractive conditions or avoiding locales of low potential and opportunity. Locally based interests may want, and most often do want, very different paths of future growth for their localities – sometimes rapid and modernising forms of growth and structural change; sometimes slow or non-existent paces of growth to preserve the qualitative dimensions that exist now without much or any future change. These national/local issues arise in virtually every country whose experience has been evaluated — whether in unitary or federal governmental systems. The key to providing effective strategies and methods of implementation for national urban growth policies is to attain political feasibility by successfully meeting the central task of reconciling the movement toward national socio-economic and environmental well-being with the attendant changes in such status for diverse localities and their populations.

Aside from 'objectively assessing' the problem conditions associated with previously discussed growth and distribution trends, the best starting place, in democratic governmental systems, to start the search for understanding of local and individual preceptions of interests is with inquiry surveys of preferences for locations in which to work, reside, recreate or establish a business. It is not a simple task to unearth what people would 'like' to do under *different* sets of circumstances, because no one operates with completely free choice and no constraints on their actions. Sometimes, it is useful to know the pure and simple essential desires of people for a living location when they do not have to worry about whether or not a job and income, educational facilities for their children, or other man-made services and amenities will be available at their ideally desired locale. But in a real world of physical and human limitations and economically scarce resources, constraints must be introduced progressively on unfettered choice to reveal the important substitutions people make in their actual location decisions and thereby inform public policy of orderings of preferences on which to base policy priorities.

10 Some Clues to Location and Life Style Preferences

Recent surveys in West Germany inquiring into location preferences for places in which to establish business and in which to reside provide the basis for some interesting and policy-relevant inferences about potential future location patterns. An employer survey conducted in 1970/71, based on a sample of 1,070 proprietors of 'footloose' consulting, research, advertising, and related types of firms from 244 places around the Federal Republic of Germany, questioned the owners of small to medium-sized firms about their overall preference for a place to establish a business and in which to live.[1] Both the positive and negative preferential attitudes were probed in the survey, with the respective resulting patterns of places preferred and places disliked for business locations shown by Figures 10.1 and 10.2. The overall complementarity of favoured and unfavoured places stands out rather clearly as the great conurbation areas of central West Germany are heavily disfavoured and selected places such as Munich, Hamburg, and Düsseldorf top a somewhat closer competiton for selection as favoured locations.

In spite of this clear overall distribution of preferences, there is a highly discriminating selective choice exercised by the respondents in the survey. Monheim attributes this to the 'image' of a place that is rooted in individual intuitive judgements of mixes of desirable and undesirable qualitative attributes. As Monheim expresses it:

> An analysis of the ideas about different places in the Federal Republic of Germany made it possible to establish which qualities have an especial influence on personal appreciation. Particularly responsible for the high number of preferences are a place's prestige, what it can offer in the way of health and recreational facilities, the charm of its landscape, its cultural and gastronomic standing, and, finally, its atmosphere, which is made up chiefly of its friendliness, attraction, many-sidedness, and its individual character. Respondents believed Munich, Hamburg, Berlin, and Düsseldorf, in particular, to possess these qualities, but mainly denied them to other places.[2]

The fairly heavy preference in favour of a supposedly attractive city such

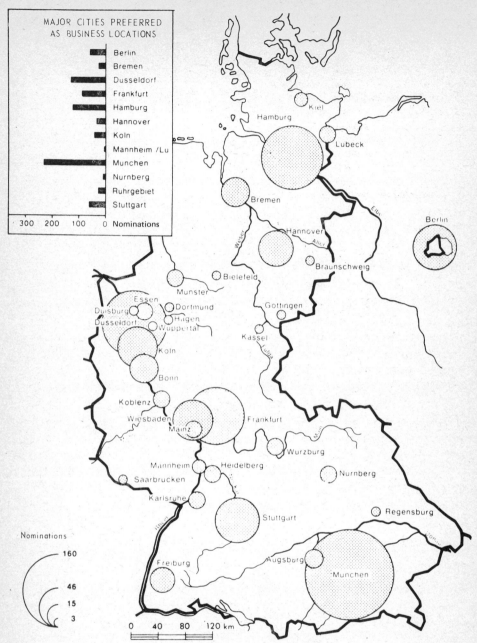

Fig. 10.1 Distribution and degree of preference for places in West Germany as business locations, 1970/71

Note: Places with more than two mentions are shown. Sizes of circles correspond to numbers of mentions.

Source: Heiner Manheim, 'Attractiveness of German towns: influences on preferences for office locations' *Informationen* vol. 15, no. 11, June 1972.

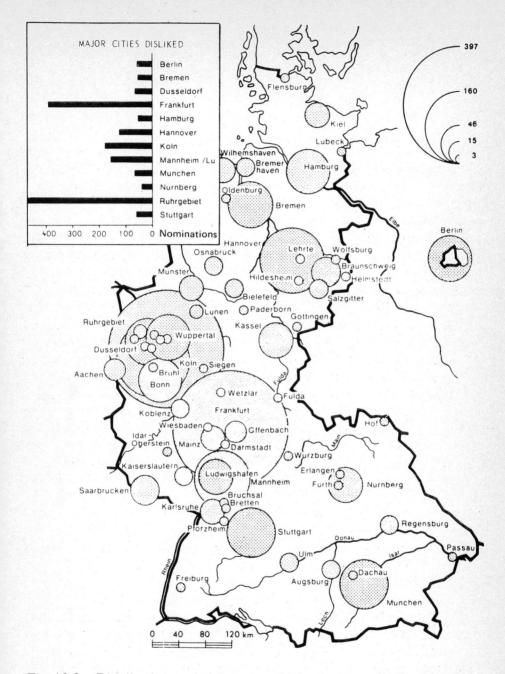

Fig. 10.2 Distribution and degree to which places are disliked in West Germany, 1970/71.

Notes: Places with more than two mentions are shown. Sizes of circles correspond to numbers of mentions.

Source: Ibid., p. 293.

as Munich which, additionally, is located within and is accessible to an extremely attractive natural environment is expectable and easily understood. A bit more surprising, perhaps, is the perceived attractiveness of a city such as Düsseldorf which is situated in a larger area, the Ruhrgebiet, that is seen by the survey respondents to be the most undesirable in all of West Germany. It is almost purely the built environment features and socio-cultural dimensions of Düsseldorf that permit its retention of a favourable image in the face of relatively more desolate surroundings. The implications of this kind of attitude toward older places undergoing structural readjustment could be of critical concern for future policy development; especially implementational approaches towards such urban areas as have at present 'poor locational images', wherein the aim is to improve critical qualitative dimensions of urban living conditions to retain present population levels, but through infusion of new population elements and shifting occupational structures that raise future socio-economic opportunity and not through mere job replacement in existing occupations.

These kinds of preferential patterns, it can be reasonably assumed, reflect the outcomes of difficult substitutions that the employers surveyed had to make between the most desirable residential and living environments and the economic requirements of profitable and competitive operation of their business enterprises, which were mainly tertiary–quaternary sector activities. As Monheim points out, 'Most of the preferences for business locations are concentrated on the conurbation areas [see Fig. 10.1]. Places with less than 500,000 inhabitants get only 16·8 per cent of the nominations; Munich is far ahead of Düsseldorf and Hamburg. Of the others, only the Rhine–Main and Rhine–Ruhr conurbations have a share of the preferences worth mentioning, while the remaining cities and other towns are largely disregarded'. Of course, it can be noted that better information for the respondents might produce a wider dispersion of preferences among other differently perceived alternative desirable locations, but there is no implication that such choice expansion would alter the distribution among *types* of areas seen as feasible business locations.

The results of another West German survey, with an entirely different set of respondents, reported in 1971, corroborates the locational orientations inferred by the employer preferences just noted.[3] Those surveyed in this second inquiry were heads of households either presently living in rural or non-urban locales or who had moved away from such localities. They were asked their preferred residential location in the event of a household move. The reponses shown in Table 10.1 are arrayed, first, by distance of the preferred location from the present residence, and, second, by the size and relative location of the preferred type of community. The

Table 10.1

Preferred type of residential location in the event of a household move,
West Germany, 1971

Preferred residential location	Percentage of those who have moved away (614 responses)	Percentage of present residents (1614 responses)
By distance from present residence		
Close proximity to present residence	25	20
In communities between 25 and 75 km.	9	9
More than 75 km.	6	5
Distance does not play role	56	51
Undetermined	4	14
By size of community		
Large cities	6	8
Peripheral communities close to large cities	30	21
Small- and medium-sized towns and cities with population of more than 10,000	33	28
Rural communities	14	11
Undetermined	17	32

Note: Responses of present and former resident heads of households of selected rural areas with economic indicators below the Federal Republic of Germany average. Based on a sample of 2,228 heads of households.
Source: Krumme, op. cit., p. 52a.

responses of those who have already moved from rural areas and those still living there are shown separately, and, while there are some differences in absolute percentages of responses falling into different distance and size categories, the distributions between categories are approximately the same for both groups of respondents.

Predominant parochial attitudes and desires for purely bucolic surroundings among even essentially non-urban residents are not borne out by these survey results. Even though between one-quarter and one-third of the respondents prefer to remain close to home, well over half would move as far as necessary to improve their residential conditions and, overwhelmingly, *not* to another rural community. Krumme observes in an understated fashion that this provides ' ... some evidence for a not insignificant latent preference for large-city proximity among the population in

Table 10.2

Factors needed to be satisfactory before moving in the
United Kingdom, 1966

Factors that would need to be satisfactory	Men	Women	Both sexes
	%	%	%
Pay and promotion prospects	62·5	56·8	61·7
Security of job	39·9	25·5	38·1
Other conditions of work	7·7	12·0	8·2
Housing	81·6	73·0	80·5
Good schools	16·0	5·4	14·6
Public transport	5·4	5·8	5·4
Shopping facilities	4·8	3·5	4·6
Social amenities	8·0	11·3	8·4
Other social characteristics of area	2·7	6·2	3·1
Amenable surroundings	16·9	18·9	17·2
Contact with friends/family	3·1	6·9	3·6
Consideration of family's wishes	2·4	0·8	2·2
Financial (other than pay)	2·2	0·8	2·0
Miscellaneous answers	0·3	0·4	0·3
No. of persons on which percentage based	1,756	259	2,015

Notes: Percentages total more than 100 because often more than one condition was mentioned.

Based on a survey of geographic labour mobility by the Government Social Survey in Great Britain.

Source: J. B. Cullingworth, *Housing and Labour Mobility,* OECD, Paris 1969, p. 39.

198

isolated, rural, low-income areas'.[4] It also provides an indication of the desirability of anticipating future urban growth needs in a way that can meet both the opportunity and amenity expectations of an urban-oriented population.

At this stage of investigation, however, one is still constrained to say that further probing of these preferential issues is a necessary, and should be a continuing, element in urban growth formulation and implementation. The factors identified in Table 10.2 as important for inducing moves by working men and women in the United Kingdom show the predominance of job and work-related factors in such decisions. Only a few other identifiable factors, such as housing, good schools, and 'amenable' surroundings, surface as important considerations. This result may derive from the fact that job security and pay rises are the only major inducements to migration, but, more likely, it emanates from the fact that a secure and growing income stream is largely a surrogate for other amenities, i.e. it provides the direct means for assuring the qualities and amounts of private and some public goods and services in the new locality. This latter may not entirely be the case but it is perhaps perceived so by the respondents.

Notes

[1] The results of the preference survey are discussed summarily in, Heiner Monheim, 'Attractiveness of German towns: influences on preferences for office locations', *Informationen* vol. 15, no. 11, June 1972, pp. 289–96.

[2] Ibid., p. 5 of an English translation (mimeo).

[3] Krumme, op. cit., p. 52.

[4] Ibid.

11   Migration, Growth and Dislocation:
Some Questions of Equity

Our discussion of the movement of people and enterprises brings us to an important feature of the phenomena with which urban growth policy deals — their dynamic nature and their manageability or potential for yielding to beneficial influence through policy intervention. As Morrison points out:

> At the present rate of migration, 6 per cent of the United States population relocates across a county line every year. Numerically, that percentage represents enough moves in five years to depopulate all 210 United States metropolitan areas with under 1 million residents and settle them anew somewhere else. The image of so many depopulated communities conveys the magnitude of migration's potential effects, but because moves are not concentrated in a few areas, this astonishing phenomenon goes largely unnoticed except in the statistics. From the personal viewpoint, after all, our cities appear settled enough. It rarely occurs to any of us that the community we live in is not so much a place as a process — a flow of people coming and going.[1]

The previously discussed systems of incentives and disincentives applied to make different urban areas and agglomerations grow relatively faster or slower operate against the backdrop of large and strongly impelled flows of people and activities. These instrument applications aim, under their respective strategies, to apply sufficient leverage to guide these flows to the ends that net accumulations and mixes of people and activities are distributed in urban localities around national territories in beneficial fashions according to the varieties of policy objectives and criteria enumerated earlier.

In earlier eras of development, the nations under evaluation here have undergone fundamental processes of industrialisation with attendant massive streams of rural to urban migration sustained over many decades that swelled cities to many times their previous sizes and created new cities where there were only villages. Countries such as the United States, Great Britain, Sweden, the Netherlands and West Germany have seen the pool of rural migrants dissipate as they have attained a stage of urban maturity wherein the major sources of urban size change come from natural increase and inter-urban migrations. France is rapidly entering this mature stage as her rural population declines to a proportion of the total comparable with these other countries.

In these earlier times of sizeable rural to urban migration the tools of urban growth policy very possibly would have proven ineffective in stemming the strong tides of population movement to the largest cities, had they been applied. In an age of mature urban systems, the issue of urban growth and distribution manageability may very likely have become a tractable one. In the United States experience, Alonso points out that with ' ... the traditional forces shrinking rapidly, intermetropolitan flows become all-important to the growth of population in diverse metropolitan areas'.[2] Further, he emphasises that 'The rate of migration to all metropolitan areas has declined from 21 per 1,000 inhabitants per year in the first decade of the century to less than 5 in 1960–1965. Migration's share of total metropolitan growth declined over this same period from 70 per cent to less than 30 per cent, and it is now apparently about 20 per cent. In other words, the intermetropolitan population system has become more closed, and changes in the structure will accordingly respond more to its internal dynamics and less to external forces'.[3]

Alonso predicts that, as a result of the drop in overall migration potential coupled with a sharp decline in the birth rate, the aggregate growth rate for all United States metropolitan areas will decline over the coming decade. Additionally, the present pattern of migration implies that at the end of the same period about one-third of these metropolitan areas will be losing population in absolute numbers. Problems of decline occurring at differing paces in larger urban areas will call for policies in the United States differing from those of the past.

As we suggested earlier, the carrying out of a policy favouring more rapid growth in some localities than in others often suffers from serious, if not fatal, political obstructions. At least with positive incentives for growth, people in certain localities are presumably happier with their lot. In cases of policy applications favouring future lower paces of growth or even absolute declines in size for an area, the situation is exacerbated by the need to avoid economic and social dislocation and, in fact, to maintain a dynamic mix of people and activities as such areas attain their new and lower growth and/or size equilibria. These latter kinds of cases may provide the ultimate tests of political feasibility and implementational ingenuity for carrying out fully symmetrical strategies that both elevate and dampen growth potentials and absolute sizes of alternative urban areas in line with national growth and distributional objectives.

The picture that emerges for countries with such mature urban systems is one in which migration flows of people and activities are still sizeable but of more moderate size, relatively speaking, than in the past and better distributed between a greater variety of urban places. This implies that instruments of policy can be applied to assist in guiding growth that is already responding to general 'trend' forces in society, e.g. the shift to relative and absolute size diminution in many larger urban agglomerations. The policy emphasis may sometimes be on accelerating the pace of growth, and at other times it may be on moderating the pace or stalling it altogether. Regardless, it may prove to be a more manageable task because the levels and forms of assistance to localities can be such as to make them somewhat more or less attractive *at the margin* for private and public location decisions. This area-based approach to balancing off relative growth potentials between alternative urban locales through selective levels and forms of public investments in them was argued for earlier on the basis of Thompson's and Berry's hypotheses of the longer-run importance of the residentiary or service sector and local infrastructure. The argument for the approach is further enchanced by Alonso's observation that the inter-urban system of places — and the places themselves we would note in addition — is, in fact, becoming more closed thereby making consistent marginal changes in such internal factors of attractiveness the more responsive points of policy leverage for producing desired longer-run diversions of population and activity flows away from or towards alternative urban locations.

Perhaps the geatest strains in policy application come from the dislocations and structural shifts in socio-economic activity and conditions in urban areas undergoing decline in size or rate of growth. Eversley's recent evaluations of the debilitating consequences of absolute population and activity declines in Greater London — attributed to an unspecified combination of general 'urban maturity trend' forces and policy constraints on growth — illustrate the nature of such problems on a grand scale.[4]

According to Eversley, primary signs of growing inequity for the remaining residents of Greater London, especially the inner boroughs of the GLC area, are the relatively diminishing real property tax base and concurrently rising tax burden, as shown by the changes in these data between 1965 and 1970 in Tables 11.1 and 11.2. The Greater London districts and other older conurbation areas virtually all experienced rises in taxable values of under 10 per cent in all use categories — with numerous percentage declines of industrial property values — while the Outer South East communities experienced rises for all uses of between 15 and 25 per cent as indicated in Table 11.1. Greater London sank noticeably below the average rates of change for all England and Wales. Further, the figures in Table 11.2 reveal that the rate of taxation applied to the taxable value base and the actual amount of tax levied per capita rose considerably more in Greater London — again, the highest percentage was for the inner boroughs — and the other older conurbation areas than they did for the Outer South East areas. These tax rate and burden changes were accompanied by population declines in the larger conurbations of between about 1 to 8 per cent, and by population increases in the Outer South East areas of almost 9 per cent.

Eversley's own summary evaluation of these changes also reveals the

Table 11.1

Current taxable value of real property in 1970 and changes in taxable values 1965–1970 in Greater London and other selected areas

Area	Total annual taxable real property value, £'000	Percentage change in taxable real property value 1965–70			
		Total	Domestic	Commercial	Industrial
England and Wales	2,440,530	13·9	16·6	14·4	7·1
Greater London	673,856	7·2	6·0	9·9	− 4·0
Inner London boroughs	369,051	6·4	5·3	7·0	−10·0
Outer London boroughs	304,805	8·2	6·5	22·3	− 0·8
Six South East Counties (Bucks, Essex, Hants, Herts, Kent, Surrey)	305,606	21·3	24·0	25·6	15·9
County boroughs (largest)					
Birmingham	53,868	8·2	11·7	8·0	− 2·9
Bristol	23,145	14·5	8·6	18·5	7·2
Leeds	22,923	11·3	9·6	14·8	4·0
Liverpool	27,847	4·9	1·9	3·7	3·8
Manchester	29,427	6·4	−3·6	9·2	− 6·7
Sheffield	24,392	16·3	22·4	21·1	2·6
South East county boroughs	88,424	11·9	9·7	13·4	7·6

Source: D. E. C. Eversley, 'Old cities, falling populations, and rising costs' *GLC Intelligence Unit Quarterly Bulletin* no. 18, March 1972, p. 9.

complexity of the compositional shifts associated with overall population decline for Greater London, as he notes that

> ... some services may be said to involve fixed costs, unrelated to resident populations; others are as much influenced by the presence, in a city, of commuting workers and tourists; others still are partly responsive to falling populations dependent on age composition changes (e.g. education); others yet may become more than proportionally cheaper as population falls (e.g. because existing buildings and plant may not require early renewal if pressure is reduced). Items like interest on past borrowing, of course, are quite unresponsive to population changes ... But in general it may be said that a city's costs are not simply population-related, so that in no case would one obtain a reduction in necessary public expenditure proportionate to the loss, for instance, from stagnant or declining domestic heriditament values. By and large, areas with growing populations show below average rises in rate burdens ... , those with declining populations show rising rate burdens [Table 11.2].[5]

It is extremely difficult to sort out the demand-related from the cost-related sources of change in levels and rates of public expenditure for these locally provided goods and services. Depending on the composition of in-land out-migrating population, Eversley asserts that 'It goes further than this. If the population which goes out is on the whole better off than those who remain behind or those who come in, the relative burden on public services may grow'.[6] He concludes, in fact, from the data in Table 11.3 showing changes in household income and its distribution between 1965 and 1970 for the GLC area as compared with the rest of the South East and the rest of Great Britain, that this is what has occurred in Greater London.

Even though these data are uncorrected for cyclical and seasonal variations, one can draw a rough inference that, by quite a large margin, household incomes in Greater London have risen relatively less on the average than those for the outer portions of the South East. In terms of income groups, both the lowest one-quarter and the highest one-quarter of wage-earning households in Greater London fared worse than the same groups in the Outer South East areas. However, the relative disadvantage of the lowest group in the GLC compared with that group in the Outer South East was nearly 23 per cent, while for the highest group it was a comparable lag of only about 7 per cent.

Eversley reads from these changes in levels and distributions of tax base, household income, and tax burden, ominous future consequences

Table 11.2

Changes in population and real property tax rate burdens in Greater London and other selected areas

Area	Population	Taxable value per capita	Tax rate applied to taxable value	Tax rates levied per capita
	Percentage change 1964–1969	Percentage change 1965/66–1970/71		
England and Wales	2·4	11·2	35·7	51·5
Greater London	−3·1	10·5	–	–
Inner London boroughs	−6·0	15·6	41·1	57·0
Outer London boroughs	−1·2	9·6	39·7	43·4
Six South East Counties (Bucks, Essex, Hants, Herts, Kent, Surrey)	8·7	11·5	28·0	41·9
County boroughs (largest)				
Birmingham	−1·8	10·1	49·6	65·4
Bristol	−1·1	15·8	40·6	58·3
Leeds	−1·0	12·5	35·4	50·5
Liverpool	−7·1	12·9	32·1	52·4
Manchester	−7·9	15·4	36·2	57·2
Sheffield	7·7	7·9	30·3	35·6
South East county boroughs	1·2	10·6	37·2	56·7

Source: Ibid., p. 10.

for Greater London in terms of its economic and social health and the fiscal ability of the Greater London Council and borough councils to provide attractive or even reasonable levels of service and environmental amenity to present and future residents. He foresees shifting population and job compositions that will produce in Greater London bi-modal distributions of low income dependent households and low-paying service jobs contrasted with high income households and quaternary jobs with very little sandwiched in between to provide the usual broad base of fiscal support and social stability. Ultimately, according to Eversley, this will produce a set of area attributes for the GLC very similar to the kinds of problems faced in some of the older conurbations in the Assisted Areas, and will call for growth assistance rather than growth constraint.

Even if we were to argue that growth constraint should not be abandoned in face of these structural dislocations perceived to be accompanying such policy, we would ignore the problems only at great peril – both in terms of the well-being of the affected residents of such an area and in terms of future credibility of urban growth policy as applied by central or federal governments in the name of national well-being. While Eversley offers some acute observations on these kinds of problems, his data and analysis only scratch at the surface and do not provide the basis for definitive conclusions on the trends he describes and about which he warns.

Table 11.3

Changes in household income and its distribution in Greater London and other areas, 1965–70

Area/Years	Percentage changes			
	Lower quartile	Upper quartile	Inter-quartile range	Median
Greater London Council				
1965–66	+ 9·1	+ 6·6	+ 4·2	+ 4·9
1966–67	+ 2·1	+ 4·4	+ 6·6	+ 4·0
1967–68	+ 5·6	+10·8	+15·2	+ 8·7
1968–69	+ 5·3	+ 9·8	+14·0	+10·8
1969–70	+ 4·9	+ 4·5	+ 4·0	+ 7·5
1965–70	+30·3	+41·5	+51·6	+41·1
Rest of the South East				
1965–66	+18·7	+19·6	+19·9	+18·5
1966–67	– 1·2	– 1·0	– 2·6	– 0·4
1967–68	+ 7·8	+ 5·6	+ 4·0	+ 9·3
1968–69	+16·6	+ 9·7	+ 4·3	+ 8·5
1969–70	+ 1·0	+ 8·2	+14·5	+11·9
1965–70	+52·5	+48·6	+45·0	+56·8
Rest of Great Britain				
1965–66	+10·8	+11·4	+12·6	+ 8·8
1966–67	+ 5·2	+ 3·6	+ 1·7	+ 4·2
1967–68	+ 1·2	+ 6·4	+11·0	+ 6·1
1968–69	+ 1·2	+ 7·4	+12·4	+ 7·3
1969–70	+ 4·2	+ 2·5	+ 1·3	+ 4·3
1965–70	+24·5	+35·2	+44·7	+34·6

Note: The original absolute values of the distribution for each year are based on gross weekly incomes reported in the Family Expenditure Survey.

Source: D. E. C. Eversley, 'Rising costs and static incomes: some economic consequences of regional planning in London' *Urban Studies* vol. 9, no. 3, October 1972, p. 360.

The significance of these concerns at present is twofold: (1) they warrant further serious and systematic investigation to define their nature in operational ways that permit appropriate linking of growth policies — aimed at constraint or stimulation — with the form and structure urban policies to which we alluded earlier; and (2) they call for a comprehensive and systematically operating set of policies to compensate people, organisations, and areas for any reasonably determined inequitable dislocations arising in the course of policy implementation that would not have occurred otherwise.

An investigation underway in the United States is addressing the very issue of the pace of growth necessary to maintain tolerable socio-economic and physical environmental balances within an urban area. Early results of a Rand Corporation analysis [7] of the City of San Jose and Santa Clara County (the surrounding hinterland), California, reveals that the expressed desires of the local populace and their governmental officials for very little or no future rise in population does indeed place residents of the area on the 'horns of a dilemma'.

Based on the econometric model constructed for the analysis, the figures in Table 11.4 show the consequences by 1980 for the unemployment rate, property value per capita index, retail sales per capita index, and level of net migration under respectively assumed annual rates of economic growth (measured by value added) of 5 per cent, rate declining from 5 to 3 per cent, rate declining from 5 to 2 per cent, and a rate of minus 1 per cent (absolute decline). Starting with the 1970 unemployment rate of about 5 per cent, it can be seen that a 5 per cent or more annual economic growth rate is required to maintain the initial conditions of 1970. Lower growth rates produce dramatic rises in unemployment and declines in the property value base. These results are not out of line with some of Eversley's conclusions on Greater London conditions under a non-growth regime. The Rand study team points out that in its work two '... alternative *a priori* hypotheses have been modelled and tested statistically. One is that private and public well-being in Santa Clara County depends only on a high, *stable* level of economic activity. The other is that such well-being depends upon a rapid rate of economic *growth*. The second hypothesis better fits the data ... '.[8]

This constitutes only the beginning of the Rand investigation. The next stage of their work explicitly focuses on the policy linkage issues between what we have termed growth and form and structure policies. As the Rand team states the case:

Since it seems clear that the County faces a dilemma over the next

Table 11.4

1980 Projections under varying growth assumptions for Santa Clara county

Assumed rate of growth of value added	Unemployment rate (per cent)		Market value of property per capita index, 1971 = 100		Retail sales per capita index, 1971 = 100		Net annual in-migration (thousands)	
	First difference model	Second difference model	First difference model	Second difference model	First difference model	Second difference model	First difference model	Second difference model
5 per cent per year	5	6	94	91	101	101	9·5	11·1
Declining, and levelling off at 3 per cent per year	8	9	87	84	100	100	3·5	8·5
Declining, and levelling off at 2 per cent per year	10	11	83	81	99	99	0·4	7·3
Minus 1 per cent per year	17	19	63	58	98	97	−10·3	5·2

Notes: Assumes 1970 labour force participation rate of approximately 40 per cent.

The first difference model employs the time-lagged rate of change in 'high technology' (e.g. aerospace) employment as the active independent variable.

The second difference model employs the time-lagged rate of change of the rate of change in such employment as the active independent variable.

Source: Urban Policy Analysis Team, *Alternative Growth Strategies for San Jose,* Preliminary Report of the Rand Urban Analysis Project, The Rand Corporation, Santa Monica, California, August 1971, p. 20.

209

ten years, the next stage of the study will examine possible ways to solve it: new types of industry which make it possible for economic well-being to be a consequence of *levels* rather than rates of change of economic activity; policies which influence development in such a way as to reduce the negative effect of growth.[9]

The questions of the degree of general validity of these kinds of growth concerns and dilemmas and the tractability of subsequently proposed policy linkages are as yet unanswered.

If the forms of future policies to avoid structural dislocations associated with growth policy implementation are yet dimly perceived, we can be reminded as well that the charters and machinery for compensating those who bear the brunt of any inevitable inequities are often weak or insufficiently framed to deal with the questions of the kind and timeliness of appropriate compensation. Action has been taken in the United Kingdom through recent presentation to the Parliament of the report on *Development and Compensation — Putting People First*,[10] to begin laying a firmer basis for the on-going process of easing adjustments that may be required in the course of executing public growth and development policies.

The initial recommendations of the report have grown out of problems related to public property takings for roads and other public works. But its purpose is to broaden the base of compensation principles and the efficient and timely application of compensatory measures for generalised applicability in most growth and development dislocations. The report starts with the very broad claim that:

> The Government are committed to enhancing the quality of everyday life in Britain. In doing so a balance must constantly be struck between the over-riding duty of the State to ensure that essential developments are undertaken for the benefit of the whole community and the no less compelling need to protect the interests of those whose personal rights or private property may be injured in the process.[11]

Specific actions to be taken in fulfilment of this pledge include: comprehensive planning and remedial measures as part of all projects and policy actions to avoid harmful effects; where damage is done in spite of these efforts reasonable compensation is to be paid; inquiry and decision on projects or policy actions and payment of any compensation due are to be made in a timely manner — based on the needs of the injured parties; and full information on the nature of public actions, an individual's rights, and any assistance available must be provided in advance in an understandable fashion. For example, cash payments to compensate for removal of a business enterprise or a household are to be made in advance of acquisition (up to 90 per cent of estimated compensation) if the proprietor or householder requires such to effect his or her move in the least disruptive manner.

These kinds of alterations in compensation rules and practices are easier to make for already established single purpose public development operations, e.g. road and motorway construction and related public works. It becomes progressively more difficult to account for and then provide commensurate compensation to alleviate the complex set of dislocations being described earlier by Eversley and the Rand team. In the latter cases, we enter into the arena of changing rules and practices of many different public bureaucracies to suit changing needs in particular urban areas over particular periods of time. Even where administratively determined changes in such things as social welfare payments, inter-governmental grants or subventions, or levels and compositions of varied public goods and services can be made, bureaucratic inertia may cause the task to seem insurmountable. Additionally, there may be changes in laws required to permit alterations in operation of affected public agencies. This means that approaches to providing such compensation flexibility and responsiveness must be well thought out in advance and changes made over a period of time in a great number of public service systems to cause them to respond in the desired way.

Notes

[1] Peter A. Morrison, 'How population movements shape national growth', The Rand Corporation, Santa Monica, California, May 1973, p. 1.

[2] William Alonso, *The System of Intermetropolitan Flows*, Working Paper no. 155, Institute of Urban and Regional Development, University of California, Berkeley, August 1971, p. 3.

[3] Ibid., p. 2.

[4] For the complete set of explanations and supporting evidence, see D. E. C. Eversley, 'Old cities, falling populations, and rising costs' *GLC Intelligence Unit Quarterly Bulletin* no. 18, March 1972, pp. 5–17; and 'Rising costs and static incomes: some economic consequences of regional planning in London' *Urban Studies* vol. 9, no. 3, October 1972, pp. 347–68.

[5] Eversley, *GLC Intelligence* ..., March 1972, p. 9.

[6] Ibid.

[7] Urban Policy Analysis Team, *Alternative Growth Strategies for San*

Jose, Preliminary Report of the Rand Urban Analysis Project, The Rand Corporation, Santa Monica, California, August 1971.

[8] Ibid., p. iii.

[9] Ibid., p. iv.

[10] Secretary of State for the Environment and the Secretaries of State for Scotland and Wales, *Development and Compensation — Putting People First*, HMSO, London, October 1972.

[11] Ibid., p. 1.

12 Conclusion: State of the Art and Future Lines of Advance

The major conclusions emerging from our foregoing evaluation of Western European and North American experience in formulating and implementing national policies and strategies for guiding urban growth can be summarised as follows:

1 The relevant geographic entities to serve as foci for urban growth policies, as opposed to other defined policies, are those delineated by the combined centripetal job/residence linkage forces and centrifugal contact intensive externality forces that result in expansion of urban areas yet cause adhesion of people and activities to a major nucleus or interlocked set of nuclei.

2 The occupational structures and thereby the socio-economic opportunity levels in such urban areas can be affected beneficially by directly guiding into or away from them, depending on under- or over-representation in alternative areas, the proportionately expanding tertiary and quaternary-sector jobs of increasingly post-industrial societies.

3 The desired distributions of people and activity between urban areas nationally, based on physical environmental criteria as well as socio-economic structural criteria, can be better ensured through chanelling infrastructural and other forms of direct public assistance in consistent ways toward alternative urban areas to raise, lower, or retain constant levels of growth potential and to provide equitable accessibility to appropriate levels and mixes of man-made and natural environmental amenity

4 The manageability and effectiveness of related policies, e.g. especially those of physical environmental protection and of socio-economic and land-use restructuring within urban areas, potentially could be enhanced through guidance of the pace and amount of growth occuring in particular urban localities over given future time periods.

5 The actual physical land area consumed in urban use remains a quite small proportion of most national land area totals even in the face of urban decentralisation and rises in urban scale, thereby giving high lever-

age to policies aimed at selecting future sites for such urban expansion, but it should be recognised that the land-using influence of urban residents is not proportional to population size and must be raised to a higher power by an exponential factor reflecting high and rising incomes that spread the burden of use more widely, e.g. through recreational extensions and vacation home sites with capital intensive development in natural areas.

6 Any set of consistent urban growth policies that pretends to measurable degrees of effectiveness and equitability should consist of components that (a) develop the core implementational activities that are concerned primarily with the aims of such policy and are necessary for its success, e.g. combined negative controls and positive inducements on private office locations for key tertiary and quaternary-sector jobs; (b) reorient all peripherally related policies that have other primary purposes in the public sector but are necessary contributors to an effective urban growth strategy, e.g. tying national government procurements and other grants or expenditures to growth-related locational criteria; and (c) strengthen existing linkages and forge new ones to complement policies that deal with the problems of adjustment and inequitability associated with differing directions and paces of growth in different locales, e.g. form and structuring policies that more efficiently relate land uses and activities within urban areas, and compensatory policies that provide monetary or in-kind (public goods and services) reimbursement or support for socio-economic and amenity inequities.

We emphasised at the beginning of our evaluation that there exists as great a need for definition of the scope and focus of what we might call national urban growth policy as for the critical analysis and evaluation of the operation and effects of such policy — this definition and subsequent evaluation is what we have attempted to supply, at least in its broader outlines. In some of the national debates on the nature of urban growth policy and the pro and con arguments for its development and application, the basic definitional issues have often become clouded with much ensuing fruitless 'tilting at windmills'.

For example, in the United States, the legislatively requested report from the Federal executive branch on urban growth policy came forth in its eventual form entitled *Report on National Growth — 1972*. In this instance, problems and policies were discussed from the standpoint of *generic* growth around the nation, i.e. rural, urban, physical, economic, and all other sorts of quantitative and qualitative change occurring in variously defined kinds of locales and regions. No set of integrated policies can be discussed sensibly if they come to mean all things to all people wherein the substantive meanings of statements and arguments are supplied willy-nilly at the discretion of all the sundry participants to the debate.

There must begin to emerge a central set of hypotheses and propositions about society, its regional and urban variations and the activities of various private and public sectors that identify and define the important relationships between the variables relevant to policy aims. This provides a testable base of public/private interaction against which to judge the validity of alternative courses of action. Urban growth policy, as we have defined it in this book, for example, then gains an identity and hypothesised mode of operation of its own for critical evaluation, refutation, and comparison with the operation of other policies.

Our own definitions have attempted to stay grounded in actual experience in the various countries and thereby not become unrealistically narrow in scope, so as to beg important policy concerns, nor become idealistically all-encompassing, and so collapse of their own weight. This has resulted in the definition and evaluation of a set of integrated policies that could (1) operate to broaden traditional regional economic policies to include social, cultural, and general amenity conditions and opportunities and reorient their application away from amorphous 'problem regions' to smaller urban locales delineated in terms of the spatial organisation of growth; and (2) operate in a complementary fashion with environmental quality and urban form and structuring policies for purposes of mutual reinforcement and synergistically produced higher levels of effectiveness.

Many recommendations for continuing innovation in the implementation of urban growth policies and strategies are self-evident from the foregoing major conclusions deriving from our analysis and evaluation. A central theme that does emerge is that future policy application could better revolve around affecting occupational structure, i.e. focus on the nature and quality of different kinds of jobs in terms of their potential for providing not only higher incomes but also greater satisfaction and range of responsibility for individuals and their families, and address meaningfully the task of offering full working and living desirability in diverse urban locales around a country. To carry out such changes more understanding is needed of public and private-sector location processes and the potential social, economic, and amenity contributions and burdens resulting from varying levels and mixes of office, industrial, and other infrastructural and public expenditure redistributions between areas.

Aside from any determinations on the substantive levels and mixes of such activity redistributions, there is also a need to concentrate in a more focused and effective way on the institutional problems of implementation. This means: (1) defining operationally the roles of the central or federal governments themselves *vis-à-vis* the roles of lower governmental levels — provinces, länder, states, and municipalities, communes, or administratively created area-based organisations; (2) identifying the key co-ordinative agencies or groups at each governmental and area level and between levels and vesting them with the appropriate operating functions and powers within respective constitutional, legal, and customary limits; and (3) establishing an on-going 'process' and capability in government at various levels, in the private sector through appropriate support, and among the affected constituencies in the population, for creating, dismantling, and creating anew the diverse implementing organisations and other mechanisms that are required, from time to time, to address particular sets of complex urban growth and development issues and to ensure effective and equitable accomplishment of desired aims.

This latter plea for a 'process' to provide flexibility over time for diverse implementational tasks, admittedly rather vague in the present writing, is based on the conviction that mechanisms for action are of use only when conceptions of problems and tasks are clear and commitment to accomplishment is forceful enough to impel their use. Past experience in the United States offers ample evidence of this set of conditions. The active use — some claim over-active use — of the legal assistance provisions of the Economic Opportunity ('war on poverty') programmes during the 1960s initiated considerable controversy because they were, in fact, effective instruments for moving governments and private citizens to action to redress the grievances of low-income and minority groups in the population. The assertion, on the other hand, that presently proposed national land use controls comprise a 'toothless lion', as noted earlier in our evaluation, rests on the argument that the substantive issues of growth are not addressed in the Federal legislation and there is little clear commitment to use of the instruments that it would provide. At the minimum, organisational instruments fashioned for carrying out urban growth policy should be rooted in the best understanding we have available of the problems confronting us, thereby yielding greater effectiveness at the time of any subsequent serendipitous 'rediscovery' of such instruments when support for their use might be forthcoming. In other words, policy implementation is better served by a minimum set of well-thought-out institutional arrangements in use or awaiting use instead of a plethora of peripherally relevant and cumbersome ones.

The level and significance of the debate on regional and urban growth policies have risen recently above the national scenes and into the international arena with the proposal for the European Community's (EEC's) regional fund.[1] The monies provided for traditional style regional economic investments would be in the form of overriding subsidies computed as percentage reimbursements on existing domestic subsidies provided in the respective EEC countries. The major arguments revolve around: (1) the amount of money to be provided in the fund; (2) whether or not the EEC should develop and fund its own projects in addition to the ones created under the domestic programmes in each country; and (3) the eligibility criteria for kinds of projects and geographical areas to be assisted along with the nature of the auditing system that will assure accountability for any and all disbursements made from the fund.

From the viewpoint of our evaluation, it is the nature of the French arguments for a smaller fund than is desired by the heavier regional spenders, e.g. the United Kingdom, Italy, the Netherlands, that are of particular interest. The French argue that, to a large extent, the effectiveness of the respective national policies rests not so much on the level of direct subsidy and infrastructural expenditure as it does on a relevant strategy – in their case an overriding urban strategy embodied in the *métropoles d'équilibre* and related city-centred orientations of assistance – that provides a workable, feasible context within which government (in this case DATAR) can negotiate the relocation from Paris of private enterprises and public agencies with minimum subsidisation. The observation that 'This has been done as much administratively as by spending money',[2] leaves one with little in the way of immediate facts and figures by which to relate 'levels' of policy action to levels of result. But it does insert into the debate the need to understand the effectiveness of *alternative* approaches and not simply to raise the ante along traditional lines of policy development.

In fairness, we must note that recent quantitative assessment of Britain's generation-long commitment to redress of traditionally perceived regional economic imbalances estimates it to have yielded measurable pay-off.[3] Perhaps of the order of 50,000 to 70,000 fewer jobs per year would have been generated in the Assisted Areas in the absence of regional subsidies, according to Brown's estimates. Other economic indicators, such as unemployment, would have been even more unfavourable than were actually experienced, and the southward migration flow would probably have been twice as large. Even with the theoretical and analytical inadequacies of his work, pointed out by Richardson,[4] and the substantive gaps in policy issues, noted by Sundquist,[5] Brown's documentation of the 'traditional alternative' as practised in Britain does offer a baseline for future comparative evaluation with other alternatives.

There exist precious few systematic quantitative analyses of even the 'hard' economic aspects, let alone the 'soft' social and political dimensions, of policy application and change in society with respect to the foregoing fields of regional and urban policies. Rather than ignoring the difficult issues, about which some kinds of decisions will have to be made, we may find it productive to move to more speculative forms of evaluation in the face of analytical intractability via more rigid scientific methods. If our assumptions are always made explicit and clear, including our value judgements, sufficient rigour may be retained to ensure logical and lucid assessment and debate of the real issues.

Regardless of the exact path of analysis and evaluation to be followed in the future, author and reader are safe in the mutual admonition that much remains to be done.

Notes

[1] 'Thompson sets a sum — and the start of a great debate' and 'The French look after their own' *The Economist,* 14 July 1973, pp. 57, 58 and 61.

[2] Ibid., p. 58.

[3] A. J. Brown, *The Framework of Regional Economics in the United Kingdom,* Cambridge University Press, Cambridge 1972.

[4] Review of Brown, op. cit., by Harry W. Richardson in *Regional Studies* vol. 7, no. 1, March 1973, pp. 109 and 110.

[5] Review of Brown, op. cit., by James L. Sundquist in *Urban Studies* vol. 10, no. 2, June 1973, pp. 277 and 278.

Index

Administrative regions (England and Wales 27
Air routes (France) 158–9
Alonso, William 202–3
Amsterdam, 17, 65
Andersson, 125
Assisted areas (UK), 15–16, 129, 165

Basildon New Town 98
Beauty, areas of outstanding natural 111
Berry, B.J.L. 19, 24, 40, 41, 47, 50, 52, 87
Birmingham 15, 52
Bonn 181–4
Bordeaux 50
Boston (Mass.) 21–2, 30, 150
Bracknell 98
Bristol 15
Brown, A.J. 217
Burlington (US) 22

Cardiff 15, 167–8
Chicago 150
Clawson, Marion 30, 31, 66
Clean Air Act (US) 115
Cleveland (US) 30
Conclusions (of this study) 213–18
Crawley 98
Cultural curve 20

DATAR (France) 131–4, 217
Des Moines 22
Dickenson, Robert 19–20

Directly Productive Activities (DPA) 123
Distribution, trends in urban 39–70
Domestic Affairs Council 77
DUS (Daily Urban Systems) 50–2, 87

Economic curve 20
Employment: imbalances in (London – 1966) 97; managerial and clerical, changes in (London) 57; patterns in (Sweden) 35, (UK) 36; rates of change in (UK) 81
Environment Protection Agency (EPA – US) 115
Equity questions 201–11
European Community's Regional Fund 217
Eversley, D.E.C. 203–7

Flemming, Sir Gilbert 165
France 19, 32, 47–50, 110–15, 126, 130–4, 156–61
Frankfurt 20–1
Future, a look at Britain's 210, 213–18

Ganser, Karl 181
Glasgow 15, 150, 167, 168, 172
Goddard, John B. 59
Göteborg 44, 52, 61, 64, 68, 178
Gottmann, Jean 31, 34, 63, 65, 68
Government Offices, relocation of: London 163–73; Stockholm

173−9; Sweden 179−81; Bonn 181−4

Greater London Development Plan (GLDP) 148

Green Belt (London) 25, 41, 53, 75, 95, 109, 110, 148

Gross Domestic Product 78

Growth sectors, working definitions of 31−7

Hague , The 17, 161

Hall, Peter 109, 110

Hansen, Niles M. 123

Hardman Report 163−8

Harlem 17

Harlow New Town 98

Hartford (US) 22

Hatfield 98

Hemel Hempstead 98

Hoch, Irving 65, 69, 70

Holiday regions (England and Wales) 26

Housing and Urban Development Act, (1970) 76

Income, tables of changes in 207

Industrial Development Certificates (IDCs) 147

Infrastructure 123, 142−3, 147−61

Instruments, range available of, generic 121−5; patterns 125−44; table of major 124

Intermediate areas (UK) 15−16

Inter-plant linkages 79−80

Jobs to men policy 125

Journeys to work 95, 101

Leavitt, Helen 115

Lever, W.F. 82−3

Life style preferences 193−9

Lille 50

Lincoln (US) 22

Location of Offices Bureau 55

London 21, 24, 26, 28, 36, 37, 39, 41, 52, 54, 65, 94−102, 163−73

Los Angeles 22, 102

Lyon 50

Malmö 44, 52, 61, 64, 68, 178

Manchester 52

Manhattan 63, 66−7

Market regions (England and Wales) 27

Marseille 50

Memphis 22

Men to jobs policy 125

Migration 40, 41, 47, 91, 201−11

Milton Keynes 165, 172

Monheim, Heiner 193, 196

Morrison, Peter A. 201

Moscow 65

Nancy 50

Nantes 50

National goals 73−7

National Labour Market Board (NLMB − Sweden) 179−80

Netherlands 17, 32, 74, 126, 143, 161

Newcastle 15

Newport (Mon.) 168

Newspaper circulation areas, importance of 20

New Towns (UK) 98

New York 21, 22, 24, 39, 63, 65, 66

Norrköping 176, 179

OECD 5

Office Development Permits (ODPs) 147, 173, 174

Offices and office jobs 53−69, 163−84

OMA (Outer Metropolitan Area,

London) 41, 42, 44, 173

Omaha 22

OSE (Outer South-East, London) 42, 43, 45, 173, 204, 205

Ottumwa (US) 22

Overhead Capital (OC) 123

Paris 18, 21, 24, 26, 39, 44, 45, 46, 47–50, 52, 68, 150

Parking problems 152–4

Planning, future public policy on 189–91

Plymouth 15, 168

Policy, objects of 15–37, 77–94

Poplar Bluff (US) 22, 24

Population, table of changes in 206

Property values 204

Prud'homme, Rémy 156

Putting People First (Dept of Environment) 210

Quaternary functions 31, 34–7, 53–69

Rand Corporation Analysis 208

,Randstad (Netherlands) 17–18, 20, 39, 74, 161

Recreational features 111

Regional Employment Premiums 129

Retirement regions (England and Wales 26

Rhineland 18, 39

Richardson, Harry W. 217

Roads (in London) 147–55; comparisons of how land used for 152

Rotterdam 17

Ruhr, The 18, 39

St Louis 22, 30

San Diego 22, 24

San Francisco 22

Santa Barbara 22, 24

Santa Clara County (US) 208–9

Selective Employment Payments Act, (1966) 129

SMSA, *see* Standard Metropolitan Statistical Area

Special Development Areas (UK) 15, 16, 129

Speed, changes in, of travel 154–5

Standard Metropolitan Statistical Area (SMSA) 27, 64, 67, 69, 85

Stevenage 98

Stockholm 21, 27, 29, 42, 44, 52, 60, 61, 173–9

Strasbourg 50

Study, purpose of this 9–11

Sundquist, James L. 217

Sweden 34, 42, 44, 46, 47, 60, 62, 73–4, 128, 134–5, 142, 173–81

Thompson, Wilbur R. 90, 93, 217

Tokyo 65

Törnquist, Gunnar 59

Toulouse 50

Transport (in London) 147–55

United Kingdom 32, 94–110, 126, 134–5, 198–9

United States 87–9, 102–4, 115, 136–40, 208; comparative regions in 28

Urban areas, working definitions of 18–31

Urban growth, trends in 39–70

Utrecht 17

Washington (DC) 21, 65, 150

Welwyn Garden City 98

West Germany 32, 80, 126, 181–4, 193–9